The Story of Our War With Spain

The Story of Our War With Spain

By

Elbridge S. Brooks

Ross & Perry Inc.
Washington, D.C.

© Ross & Perry, Inc. 2001 All rights reserved.

No claim to U.S. government work contained throughout this book.

Protected under the Berne Convention. Published 2001

Printed in The United States of America
Ross & Perry, Inc. Publishers
717 Second St., N.E., Suite 200
Washington, D.C. 20002
Telephone (202) 675-8300
Facsimile (202) 675-8400
info@RossPerry.com

SAN 253-8555

Library of Congress Control Number: 2001093133

http://www.GPOreprints.com

ISBN 1-931641-40-4

♾ The paper used in this publication meets the requirements for permanence establishe the American National Standard for Information Sciences "Permanence of Paper for Prir Library Materials" (ANSI Z39.48-1984).

All rights reserved. No copyrighted part of this publication may be reproduced, stored in retrieval system, or transmitted, in any form or by any means, electronic, photocopying, recording, or otherwise, without the prior written permission of the publisher.

SIGSBEE LEAVING THE MAINE.
("I suggested the propriety of my being the last to leave.")

(See page 34.)

PREFACE

In this story of our war with Spain no attempt has been made to enter upon a discussion of methods or an elaborate plan of campaign.

The author's design has been to give simply, concisely, and connectedly the complete story of what President McKinley calls "our extraordinary war with Spain," so that readers, young and old, who have neither time nor inclination for the study of operations in too great detail may obtain, as it were, a bird's-eye view of the war from the insistent causes to the final triumphal close.

Besides Mr. Emerson's spirited drawings, the publishers were able to procure from one of the "boys" actually at the front "snap shots" of prominent scenes and places that add a distinctive value to the story, and make privation, action, and environment even more real than could a mere "hearsay" sketch. Thanks also are due to Mr. Wendell Phillips Thoré for assistance and suggestion.

E. S. B.

BOSTON, March 17, 1899.

CONTENTS

CHAPTER		PAGE
I.	Why the *Maine* was in Havana Harbor	9
II.	Why Congress gave the President Fifty Millions	27
III.	How the War began	49
IV.	How Admiral Dewey spent his May-day	66
V.	Why the United States Navy played at Hide-and-seek	90
VI.	How they bottled up the Spanish Fleet at Santiago	111
VII.	How the Marines held the Beach at Guantanamo	130
VIII.	Why the Boys cheered at Daiquiri	150
IX.	How they cleared the Jungle at Guasimas	165
X.	How they broke the Line at El Caney and stormed the Hill of San Juan	181
XI.	How they surprised the Governor of Guam	201
XII.	How the Spanish Admiral made a Dash for Liberty	221
XIII.	Why they cheered in the Trenches	245
XIV.	How the Flag floated over Porto Rico	262
XV.	Why General Merritt played Jackson at Manila	280
XVI.	The Things that helped	296
XVII.	How the War ended	317

The Story of our War with Spain chronologically told . . 337

LIST OF ILLUSTRATIONS

	PAGE
Sigsbee leaving the *Maine*	*Frontispiece*
A Bit of Old Havana	9
The Landing-place of Columbus	11
Arms of the Conquistadores	14
On the Plaza de Armas, Havana	17
The Wall at Santiago	20
The Morro, Havana	23
President McKinley	27
The U.S. Battleship *Maine*	31
A Cuban Farm-house	36
Spanish Troopers	41
The Home of a Sugar Planter	44
Near Matanzas	51
A Cuban Soldier	59
A Typical Farm-house	61
View from the Yumuri Valley, near Matanzas	64
Admiral Dewey	66
On Corregidor Island	69
Dewey at Manila	79
Rear Admiral Sampson	90
The Transports en route to Cuba	92
The City of Cadiz in Spain	95
The Diamond Rock, off Martinique	101
The Harbor of San Juan in Porto Rico	105
The *New York*	107

LIST OF ILLUSTRATIONS

	PAGE
Lieutenant Hobson	111
In the Harbor of Santiago	113
Cabanas	118
Hobson on the Bridge of the *Merrimac*	125
Where the *Merrimac* lies	129
Hobson's Interpreter	132
The Marines at Guantanamo	139
Morro Castle, Santiago	145
General Shafter	150
At the Dock at Tampa	154
The Heights of Jibara	157
Baracoa, near Cape Maisi	159
Colonel Roosevelt	165
Spanish "Fortine," or Fort No. 1, outside of Santiago	167
The Jungle Path at Guasimas	172
Camp of the Rough Riders	176
The Road to El Caney	183
Where the Right Wing marched	185
"Capron's Pet"	187
After the Battle	190
The San Juan River	192
The Charge up San Juan Hill	195
The Reserves waiting for Orders	199
Where Guam is	203
"The Silent Gun"	208
The U.S. Cruiser *Charleston*	211
In Philippine Waters	214
Admiral Schley	221
Trench-making before Santiago	222
Camp of the American Advance	224
The Inner Harbor of Santiago	227
Where Cervera ran out	231

LIST OF ILLUSTRATIONS

	PAGE
Wainwright on the *Gloucester*	237
U.S. Cruiser *Brooklyn*	241
Bamboo Bridge over the San Juan River	246
In the Trenches	248
A Silk-cotton Tree	251
Mule Train on the Way to relieve the Santiago Refugees	252
The Church at El Caney	253
Railway Station on the Road from El Caney to Santiago	256
"No Cheering!"	259
General Miles	262
A Bullock Cart in Porto Rico	264
The Casa Blanca	267
A Porto Rican Garden	271
A Mountain Battery	274
"Cease firing! Peace has been declared!"	277
The Approach to Manila	285
A Street in Manila	291
"Capron's Pet"	298
A Noble Helper	302
The *St. Paul* and *The Terror*	305
"Taking his Quinine"	310
Supplies for the Camp	315
Santiago Harbor and the Morro	318
Bridge on the El Caney Road	321
In Santiago	324
At Montauk	327

THE STORY OF
OUR WAR WITH SPAIN
IN 1898

THE
STORY OF OUR WAR WITH SPAIN

CHAPTER I

WHY THE MAINE WAS IN HAVANA HARBOR

A BIT OF OLD HAVANA.

AT midday on Tuesday, the twenty-fifth of January, 1898, the United States battleship *Maine* steamed into the harbor of Havana, the chief city of the Spanish island of Cuba. Spotless and speckless from keel to fighting-top, with the Stars and Stripes at the peak and the Jack at the foremast head, the great white cruiser, guided by a Spanish pilot, threaded the narrow entrance to the harbor, and just abreast the Admiral's Palace, on the water-front of the Cuban metropolis, ran out her chains and made fast to the mooring-buoy selected by the Spanish pilot. Then her guns thundered their salute to the Spanish flag, the naval cadet reported to the American consul, and Yankee commander and Spanish admiral exchanged visits of courtesy.

At forty minutes past nine on the night of Friday, the fifteenth of February, 1898, without warning and apparently without reason, while lying peacefully in the same mooring-berth to which the Spanish pilot had conducted her, the United States battleship *Maine* blew up with a bursting, rending, crashing roar, and two hundred and fifty-four Yankee blue-jackets went down in the blackness and smoke of the ruined battleship to swift and sudden death in the harbor of Havana.

"Well, what business had she there, anyhow?" certain faultfinding and unpatriotic Americans demanded, when the world fell to discussing this baffling and awful disaster.

What business had that armed battleship of the United States in the unfriendly but not openly hostile waters of Havana? Let us first discover this before we chronicle the results of that terrible catastrophe which precipitated a peaceful, home-loving people into a foreign and aggressive war, and wrung from American lips, from ocean to ocean and from Lakes to Gulf, the stern and determined watchword: "Remember the *Maine!*"

WHY THE MAINE WAS IN HAVANA HARBOR

The reason for the presence of the *Maine* in Spanish waters dates far back in the history of America.

From the days of Columbus, the admiral, who first planted upon American soil the yellow banner of Spain, that emblem of discovery, occupation,

THE LANDING-PLACE OF COLUMBUS.
(At the north end of Watling's Island, one of the Bahama group.)

colonization, and conquest had been also the symbol of inhumanity, selfishness, and greed.

There had been notable exceptions to this record of tyranny, from the noble Las Casas, "protector of the Indians," to the gentle Fray

Junipero Serro, friend of the California tribes; but the exceptions only helped to prove the rule. The methods of Spain in America were those of mediæval times, and the customs of Spain in her colonies were, in 1800, not a day advanced beyond the Middle Ages — the times of Alva and the Inquisition, of Pizarro and Cortes and De Soto. From the very beginning of Spanish occupation, therefore, the hand of Spain lay heavy upon the vast American empire that Columbus and his successors had delivered into her keeping.

This "empire" embraced the greater part of Central and South America, the fertile islands known as the West Indies, and all that section of what is now the United States of America lying west of the Mississippi.

This portion of North America, of especial interest to us, Spain took to herself through those unjust and unwritten laws of discovery, exploration, and conquest that were a part of the law of nations four centuries ago, as they are to-day to an only slightly modified extent.

By the right of discovery and exploration Spain claimed North as well as South America. For her ships and sailors had carried into northern as well as southern waters the proud banner of

Castile; it had floated on the St. Lawrence and the Hudson, in the harbor of Plymouth and above the long reaches of Chesapeake Bay, while traces of Spanish occupancy exist in Maryland and Virginia and reach far into the interior of New York state. De Soto and his men zigzagged across the Southern states from Pensacola in Florida to New Orleans, now wandering as far north as the James River and now as far south as Mobile Bay, ending finally at Vicksburg, from which they drifted dismally down the Mississippi to disaster and death. Coronado and his glittering train of armored men wandered from Mexico to Kansas, and, on a fruitless hunt for storied cities, walled in gold and gems, doomed to disappointment, left their traces in the conquered pueblo of Santa Fé in New Mexico, which divides with St. Augustine in Florida (both Spanish settlements) the honor of being the oldest city in the United States.

By virtue of Spanish discoveries before the days of Sebastian Cabot, Spain disputed with England the right of possession, and that dispute, inherited by the United States from England, has rankled and smouldered through all the years since first England and Spain struggled for the mastery of the western world.

The Spaniards, to be sure, never extended their encroachments or actual demands north of Delaware Bay; but, from the first presence of Englishman and Spaniard upon the waters and within the limits of the New World, this strife for possession was sure to come. Indeed, in the settlement of America, the newly found lands fell largely to Spain and England, and as the Anglo-Saxon race spread itself along new lines of occupation and conquest, the Spaniards in North America found themselves confined to the banks of the Mississippi and the shores of the Gulf of Mexico. Had all Spanish governors possessed the ability of Galvez or the courage of young Louis Grandpré, whose story all American boys should read, the records of the struggle with Spain would have been quite different from

ARMS OF THE CONQUISTADORES.
(Toledo blades and Spanish cutlass, used in the "colonization" of the West Indies. From San Domingo.)

WHY THE MAINE WAS IN HAVANA HARBOR 15

what they are, although the result would have been the same; for the American race of Anglo-Saxon strain would at last have possessed itself of the whole southern and western country, though forty times the strength of Spain barred the path to progress and expansion.

Theodore Roosevelt makes the three great stages in the advance of the Anglo-Saxon race the conquest of Britain, the defeat of the Spanish Armada, and the establishment of the United States. In the last two of these three stages, Spain was a leading factor; for the West, though won from England, was equally won from Spain.

The continued and overmastering pressure of the American frontiersman, pioneer, and colonist could not be withstood by the less aggressive and more dilatory Spanish officials in the south and southwest. But, now and then, a flash of the old-time Spanish valor lights up the story, as when the intrepid Galvez, a youthful and brilliant soldier, swept the Mississippi of British and Americans, and laid successful siege to Mobile and Pensacola; or as when the Spanish captain Pierro led a successful invasion and foray from St. Louis to the Lakes and planted the banner of Spain in the heart of what is to-day the city of Chicago.

These were but flashes of spirit, however, which flickered and died out before the resistless advance of the hardy American borderers, and when Thomas Amis with his flatboat tried to force the Spanish lines at Natches, and George Rogers Clark in 1786 raided the Spanish merchants at Vincennes, it was the entering wedge that led at last to the giving up by Spain of the vast region beyond the Mississippi, the stern "clearing up" by Jackson in Florida, and the final withdrawal of the Spaniard from the land above which from the days of De Soto and Coronado the yellow standard of Spain had floated in possession, and in which she had won and lost an empire.

The story of Spanish intrigue for power and possession in North America played a more important part in the greater story of the United States than our histories admit; it has, indeed, no small bearing upon our long and unsettled relations with Spain. That nation never had sympathy or affection for the United States. Her apparent willingness to help the colonies in their struggle for independence was altogether selfish and by no means real. It was because she hated England, an old-time foe, not because she loved America, her would-be ally; and, all through the

American Revolution and the unsettled days that followed, Spain's relations with the United States were marked by insincerity and double-dealing.

ON THE PLAZA DE ARMAS, HAVANA.
(Formerly the palace of the Governor-General of Cuba.)

At last she was forced off the mainland and into the sea, occupying as her last foothold those beautiful islands which she had misgoverned and wasted for centuries, known as the Antilles or, as Americans termed them, the West Indies. Her possessions in Central and South America dropped from her, one by one, until at last, of all her once glorious colonial empire, only Cuba and Porto Rico acknowledged the overlordship of the Spanish flag.

For years too, even in those "ever faithful isles," as Spain loved to term them, faithfulness was scarcely to be relied upon, and the flag of Spain remained with but uncertain tenure. Spain learned nothing by experience, and her government of her last remaining islands was marked by the same arrogance, greed, and cruelty that had deprived her of all those vast possessions in America that had once been hers.

As the nearest power and the natural commercial neighbor of Cuba and Porto Rico, the United States was again and again brought into unpleasant relations with Spain. To the great republic those islands looked for trade, to it they turned for countenance and support in every futile effort they made for relief or independence.

From 1823 to 1868 — nearly fifty years of uneasiness — these restless Cuban revolts against Spain were little more than "disturbances"; but in that year began the ten-years war. It was the first concerted movement for actual independence.

The territory of the United States was only a hundred miles away; it was the natural shelter for large numbers of Cuban refugees or sympathizers, and it naturally became the "outfitting" place for frequent unauthorized attempts at armed help to the Cuban rebels. These expeditions, being unlawful, were prohibited by the United States; but they were secretly promoted and prepared nevertheless, and though some of these filibusters were restrained or arrested, certain of their expeditions did slip away from American vigilance, and land their men and war material in Cuba.

One such filibustering expedition, embarked upon a small American sidewheel steamer named the *Virginius*, slipped away in October, 1873, escaping American supervision, and with arms and men on board fell into the hands of the Spaniards. At once, the one hundred and thirty-five men captured on the *Virginius* were, with customary Spanish cruelty, declared "pirates," and fifty-three of them, without trial and in spite of the protests of the American and British consuls, were taken ashore at Santiago, ranged up against a wall, still known as the place of martyrdom, and were there inhumanly shot.

Certain of these men were American citizens, and, although by being engaged in an unlawful enterprise which their own government had prohibited and threatened with punishment, they were taking their lives in their hands, still so brutal and summary a proceeding could not go unnoticed, and the United States was at once horrified and indignant.

This indignation very nearly ripened into war. Indeed, actual conflict was only averted by Spain's official and complete apology, including a money indemnity and a salute to the American flag; but

THE WALL AT SANTIAGO.

(Along this wall the *Virginius* prisoners were ranged and shot in 1873.)

even this did not satisfy the great body of Americans, who felt that Spain's apology was as insincere as its methods, and believed, with Secretary Fish and President Grant, that this was only a postponement of the inevitable conflict.

This conflict, in fact, was becoming more and more certain. For over seventy years the possession of Cuba by Spain had been a menace and an eyesore to the United States. The methods of government, the treatment of the people, the continual restlessness and unhappiness of the Cubans, the ineffectual efforts toward settlement or pacification, the frequency and annoyance of filibustering schemes, the arrogance of Spain, all combined to urge the United States to some attempt at settling the Cuban problem, which had indeed been a problem ever since the declaration of the Monroe Doctrine in 1823, and the plan for the annexation of Cuba in 1840.

More than this, the business interests of the United States in Cuba were constantly increasing; American citizens, resident there because of business duties, were continually in danger or jeopardy; and, more important still, the miserable and insufferable sanitary conditions of what should be a healthful and beautiful island made the land a breeding-spot of yellow fever and other menacing diseases to which almost every epidemic that had visited the United States could be directly traced.

In spite of all this, however, peace with Spain would have remained unbroken had not a new outburst of the rebellious spirit led to the revolt from Spain which began in February, 1895. This led to a wasting and ineffectual war which brought victory neither to Spanish masters nor Cuban rebels, but did materially weaken and destroy the industries of the island, especially the large sugar trade in which the United States was directly interested. Added to this were the brutal and mediæval methods to which the Spanish governor, General Weyler, resorted to overcome and kill off the Cuban non-combatants; these were known as "reconcentrados."

"Weyler's plan" was, in fact, nothing less than a process of slow starvation, and it awakened the indignation of all Americans who believed in humanity and fair play. This American dissatisfaction led, in 1896, to an advance on the part of Congress, requesting the President of the United States to make some move toward stopping this critical and horrible condition of affairs in Cuba; but nothing was actually done except that President Cleveland, in his Annual Message of December, 1896, referred to Spain's "inability" to deal successfully with the insurrection, and declared that "a situation will be presented in which our obligation to the sovereignty of Spain will be superseded by higher obligations which we can hardly hesitate to recognize and discharge."

WHY THE MAINE WAS IN HAVANA HARBOR 23

This meant that if Spain did not act better and "play fair" toward her persecuted Cuban subjects, the United States could not stand it longer, and would have to interfere, in the interests of humanity, decency, order, and justice.

This was the condition of affairs when William McKinley became President of the United States by the election of 1896. Starvation, desolation, destruction, and inhumanity were ruining one of the fairest islands of the world — an island which, from the time the Spaniards had discovered and occupied it, had never been allowed a fair chance

THE MORRO, HAVANA.

(The old castle guarding the entrance to the harbor which the *Maine* saluted in passing.)

to successfully develop its great resources or lift its people above the rank of vassals and slaves.

More and more the tendency of public opinion in America was toward interference. This displayed itself in every way, from a friendly suggestion to Spain to the recognition of the rights of the rebels, acknowledgment of the Cuban Republic, and armed invasion by the forces of the United States. Hotheads in Congress and irresponsible newspapers throughout the Union exerted themselves to rouse the President and the people to some radical and determined action. But the United States never did care to meddle with the affairs of other nations; the United States is a peace-loving nation and abhors war, in which it has had repeated and harsh though always victorious experiences. So, when the Spanish government recalled the cruel and brutal Governor Weyler, put in his place the more humane Governor Blanco, promised reform in its government of the Cubans, and promised also that the loyal Cubans should be allowed to govern themselves under much the same system as the British subjects of Canada and Australia, the President and people of the United States said, "We will wait awhile longer, before doing anything," — and waited, hoping for better things.

But better things did not come, as promised or as hoped. Indeed, the self-governing scheme proved an utter failure; the miserable "reconcentrados" were neither released nor relieved, and an opposition to the new methods, led on by Spanish soldiers and officials, provoked frequent outbreaks and open riot even in Havana itself.

In July, 1896, Major-General Fitzhugh Lee, a Virginian of proved ability and courage, was sent to Havana as Consul-General of the United States. He found the island ground beneath the double burdens of Spanish taxes and Spanish tyranny; as victims of the latter were numerous naturalized citizens of the United States, against whose arrest and punishment the Consul-General vigorously protested; he found the "home-rule" reforms of the Spaniards little more than a farce, while the pitiable condition of the unfortunate "reconcentrados" was only very slightly relieved by the help sent in money and supplies from the United States; he found that the rebels of the island were proof against the bribery and the questionable truce or armistice proffered by the Spanish Governor-General, while the officials and army officers of Spain were abetting the riotous and unsettled conditions of Havana, to the great danger and positive threatening of the American residents.

It was clear to General Lee that some demonstration of interest in behalf of these endangered

Americans was necessary on the part of the United States, especially as it appeared as if Governor-General Blanco might not be able to "control the situation," as he expressed it.

He therefore suggested that a naval vessel of the United States be made ready to "move promptly in case American interests in Cuba suffered because of our open sympathy with the starving Cubans"; and for that reason the battle-ship *Maine* was ordered to Havana; for this reason on the fifteenth of February the *Maine* lay at her moorings in Havana harbor.

CHAPTER II

WHY CONGRESS GAVE THE PRESIDENT FIFTY MILLIONS

PRESIDENT McKINLEY.

THE appearance of the battleship *Maine* in Havana harbor did not please the Spaniards of Cuba. Naturally they could not, in their excited condition, look upon the coming of such a warship at such a time as altogether the "friendly naval visit" it was announced to be. Indeed, Consul-General Lee himself, in view of the unfriendly and hostile feeling that had increased toward Americans during the days of the disturbed and riotous condition of Havana, felt that it would be well to postpone the visit a few days and give the excitement time to disappear.

His telegram of advice, however, came too late; for the Secretary of State advised him that the

Maine had already been ordered to proceed to Havana, and the very next morning the big white battleship sailed into Havana harbor, and proceeded to the mooring-berth assigned her by the harbor master.

For three weeks she lay thus at anchor. Her officers received and returned the official visits that are the rule in all ports entered by warships in time of peace, but Captain Sigsbee of the *Maine* was convinced and, in fact, was made to feel that there was no real friendliness on the Spanish side in this exchange of courtesies. Under all the pleasant speeches there was, he saw, a spirit of resentment and unfriendliness toward Americans. Anxious to avoid any opportunity for disturbance, the captain kept his crew on board, not granting them the "shore leave" customary when vessels are in port. He put them through all the regular ship drills, excepting "night quarters" and "clearing for action," but he was careful to avoid everything that might be misrepresented or misjudged.

While the *Maine* floated thus at her mooring-berth at Havana, a foolish piece of work on the part of the Spanish minister was performed at Washington. This careless official, whose duty it was to be very particular in his actions, wrote a

WHY CONGRESS GAVE FIFTY MILLIONS

letter to a friend in which he went out of his way to misjudge, belittle, and insult President McKinley. A Cuban spy whose chief aim was to embroil Spain and the United States obtained possession of this letter, and placed it in the hands of the Cuban Agents, or "Junta," in New York, who, in turn, gave it to a New York newspaper anxious for sensations. The letter was published and did create a sensation. It made Americans indignant, caused the immediate resignation of the Spanish minister, and still further complicated matters already unsettled because of the Cuban trouble.

It was while this bit of comedy was being played that the chief tragedy of the war was enacted in Havana harbor. It was on the evening of the fifteenth of February. The Spanish minister had resigned and left the country; the American people were divided between amusement and indignation; the Spaniards in Cuba were infuriated over the fact that the minister had been found out, and, in their anger at the Americans — "the Yankee pigs," as they loved to call us — and at the presence of an American warship in Havana harbor, they had taken to sending threatening letters and circulars to the cool Consul-General Lee and the equally cool Captain Sigsbee; and the tenor of these letters was "the moment of action has arrived. Death to the Americans!"

It was past nine o'clock; the *Maine* was swinging at her mooring-buoy; the captain was writing in his cabin; the bugler was sounding taps:— "turn in and keep quiet;" the cabin mess-attendant had taken up his banjo after looking after the captain's wants, and the big ship was just settling itself for the night, heading north and west in the windless current exactly in position to rake the shore fortifications had she been on a warlike mission and "cleared for action."

The night was dark and overcast, hot and sultry; the steam launch was riding at the starboard boom; the crew had turned in; the quarter-watch was on duty; the officers were in their mess-room, and everything, apparently, was quiet and peaceful on ship and shore.

Suddenly, into the sultry night, boomed a dull, muffled explosion, as if smothered by water; then came a bursting, rending crash followed by a dull red glare. It splintered, ripped, and tore; the air was filled with missiles and flying timbers; the electric lights went out; the great vessel trembled, lurched, and listed to port; then the bow, raised above the waves a moment, went down head first;

THE U.S. BATTLESHIP MAINE.

the water rushed in through the great holes torn in the shattered hull; and two hundred and fifty-four men — for the most part sleeping sailors in their quarters on the berth-deck — were carried down to death in the torn and shapeless wreck of the splendid battleship *Maine* — once the pride of the noble White Squadron of the American navy.

Offers of help and ready assistance came at once from the Spanish war-vessels and other ships in the harbor. Regrets and sympathy with assurances of the absolute ignorance on their part of the cause of the terrible disaster came from Spanish officials on ship and shore. But the fact remained that the *Maine* had been blown up while moored by a Spanish pilot to a Spanish buoy in a Spanish harbor; and to this day, though the cause of the explosion remains a mystery, the combination of suspicious circumstances has impressed upon the American people that their splendid warship was deliberately destroyed for hostile reasons by the hostile people who resented its presence in a Spanish port.

The total death roll of that night of horror (including the injured who died on shore) was two hundred and sixty-four men and two officers; and for that sacrifice Spain has been held to strict account and has paid for it dearly in blood and land and treasure. For, argue it as we may, if the *Maine* had not been blown up in Havana harbor, the war with Spain might, for a time at least, have been averted.

But even the terrible tragedy of the *Maine* did not at once "let slip the dogs of war," as Shakespeare puts it. The great good sense of the American people, which can always be relied upon in critical moments, again asserted itself in spite of the demands for vengeance that came from over-excitable citizens and sensation-seeking newspapers. With a marvellous patience and a splendid

WHY CONGRESS GAVE FIFTY MILLIONS

restraint the American people awaited the verdict of the Naval Court of Inquiry which was at once appointed by the President to investigate and report upon the cause of the destruction of the *Maine*.

This example of restraint was set by those officials upon whom action depended. In the midst of sorrow, loss, wrath, and wreck Captain Sigsbee of the foundered *Maine*, realizing that the patience of the people was well-nigh exhausted and that unwise words might lead to regrettable results, sank his own feelings and suspicions and, in telegraphing to Washington the tidings of the fearful disaster, made no charges, but begged that "public opinion should be suspended until further report."

To one who calmly reads those words to-day, apart from the terrible strain under which they were written, their full significance can scarcely be appreciated. The last man to leave the cruel wreck of his noble ship, Captain Sigsbee could still repress his wrath and command his sorrow even though he felt certain as to the cause of the disaster and the responsibility for the murder of his men.

"It was a hard blow to be obliged to leave the *Maine*," he says, "and we waited until we were satisfied that she rested on the bottom of the harbor. Lieutenant-commander Wainwright then directed everybody to get into the boats — an easy operation; one had only to step directly from the deck into the boat. I suggested the propriety of my being the last to leave and requested my officers to precede me, which they did."

Fifteen minutes after his sad leave-taking of the stranded *Maine*, in which had gone to death, as Captain Sigsbee bears witness, "as worthy and true patriots as those we have lost in battle, but whose fate was an even sadder one," the commander of the *Maine* had sent his famous despatch, which announced the disaster and restrained the hot wrath of a nation.

The attitude of President McKinley, also, — cool, calm, and deliberate, peace-loving, but loving justice more than all — strengthened what the President himself characterized as "the sturdy good sense of the national character" as well as its own "instinct of justice," and held it curbed and silent until the Board of Inquiry made public its decision.

This decision came after the deliberations of the commission or Board of Inquiry, which had been in session for twenty-three days in Havana harbor and at Key West. It was the result of a careful and complete examination, in which, however, it must be said Spain had no opportunity to present her side of the case. The finding of the Board declared that the *Maine* was exploded by a submarine mine; but how this was done, by whom placed and when, by whom set off and how, the Board could not decide through lack of positive testimony, and the mystery of the *Maine* is still an unexplained and unfathomed problem. But by the people of the United States the responsibility for the tragedy which slaughtered two hundred and sixty-four American blue-jackets in the harbor of Havana was sternly and righteously placed upon the nation which should have been a generous host rather than a diabolical destroyer, and upon Spain, and Spain alone, rests the responsibility for the terrible cry, "Remember the *Maine*," which, more than philanthropy, more than humanity, more than love of liberty even, drove a peaceful nation into war and brought a proud kingdom to disaster, dismemberment, and loss.

But it was not alone this fierce and bitter cry for justice that drove the republic into war. While the loss of the *Maine* touched the great heart of the people even more than the woes of reconcentrados and the struggle of patriots, the claims of humanity and protection joined hands with impatience and commercial interest, and set afoot a widespread public demand for some immediate and definite action. It filled the press with clamor, captured the Congress by its persistency, and bore with tremendous force upon the President, to whom the will of the people must be the supreme law.

A CUBAN FARM-HOUSE.
(The home of the reconcentrados.)

William McKinley saw that a crisis was at hand; he knew that war was inevitable; but he knew, too, that to precipitate the country, unprepared for hostilities, into the unknown disturbances and possibilities of a foreign war, might be fraught with the gravest dangers to the republic. But the President

WHY CONGRESS GAVE FIFTY MILLIONS

was by nature shrewd as well as sagacious, politic as well as patriotic, deliberate as well as determined. Before the loss of the *Maine* he had felt that actual hostilities might be averted and that the calm methods of diplomacy might secure the ends he had in view. But the destruction of the *Maine* changed this. It shut all the avenues of action save one — and that one was war.

But William McKinley had been a soldier himself in the greatest of all American conflicts. He knew what war meant; he knew, too, what an unreadiness for war meant to a nation, which, at peace for thirty-three years, rushed into strife without forethought and marched to battle without preparation.

Hotheaded and unreasoning men who developed a sudden and feverish patriotism united with newspapers as choleric and overheated, and charged the President with hesitancy and indecision, because he did not at once fill Cuba with soldiers he did not have and invade Spanish territory with ships and sailors that must be rubbed into existence as suddenly and miraculously as with Aladdin's lamp.

War was inevitable, but delay was preparation. A vast seacoast lay almost totally undefended against the invasion of a foreign power; the regular fighting force of the United States Army was far below the smallest limit, and the militia was by no means on a war footing.

So, while saying in his message to Congress which, on the twenty-eighth day of March made public the finding of the Board of Inquiry, " I do not permit myself to doubt that the sense of justice of the Spanish nation will dictate a course of action suggested by honor and the friendly relations of the two governments," President McKinley himself determined to forestall that course of action by making ready for whatever might happen, remembering the words of Washington: " To be prepared for war is one of the most effectual means of preserving peace."

It is well that the boys and girls of America who, later, must study and take to heart the events that made the year 1898 historic should consider the task which had fallen to William McKinley as the chief executive—the responsible head of the republic. He must not only ignore politics and keep the nation from being divided in opinion, but he must at the same time put on foot preparations for an unknown and possibly wide-reaching war demanding the services of hundreds of thousands of fighting men; he must not only prevent European interference and meddling, perhaps open hostility, but he must delay the actual shock of war until the American Army and Navy, recruited from an unwarlike people, could be put into some sort of readiness and discipline, and he must, above all, so hold and handle the Congress that it should neither force an unwise recognition of the shadowy Cuban republic, a sudden and unsupported declaration of war, nor a hopeless division of action by the lack of executive decision and will.

All of these mighty "musts" the President of the United States did perform, and he performed them so calmly, so deliberately, so sagaciously, and yet so quietly but firmly, that the spectacle was presented to the world of an absolutely united and patriotic Congress, composed of varying and even antagonistic political elements, responding, without a word of objection, to the President's suggestion of his needs, and placing in his hands by the magnificent vote of 311 to 0 in the House of Representatives and also by a unanimous vote in the Senate the sum of fifty millions of dollars "for the national defence and for each and every purpose connected therewith, to be expended at the discretion of the President." It was a superb recognition of the republic's trust in the man within whose hands it had placed the direction of its affairs.

The President was overjoyed at this mark of confidence, but he appreciated the fact that this act of providing for possibilities came none too soon. "Our coasts," he has since explained, "were practically undefended; our navy needed large provision for increased ammunition and supplies and even numbers to cope with any sudden attack from the navy of Spain, which comprised modern vessels of the highest type of continental perfection; our army also required enlargement of men and munitions."

We are too apt to think that Spain was a foeman scarce worthy of our steel; but this is neither just nor true. Spain had been a fighting nation for a thousand years; she was on a continual "war footing," always ready for assaults, rebellions, or defence; had she taken advantage of her possibilities, she might have made a sudden and disastrous descent upon our defenceless coasts, for her navy, as the President declares, comprised some most formidable fighting ships, and she had in the islands of Cuba and Porto Rico nearly two hundred thousand armed and disciplined soldiers.

WHY CONGRESS GAVE FIFTY MILLIONS

Against this force the United States had a regular army of less than twenty-five thousand men, while the militia of the several states though considerable in numbers was ill-prepared for the actual state of war; the navy, too, needed strengthening alike in ships and men, although the remarkable discipline of years of peace, thanks to a wise super-

SPANISH TROOPERS.
(As seen in the streets of Santiago.)

intendence of naval affairs, had brought its marines and blue-jackets to a surprising scale of precision and perfection.

So, with fifty millions of dollars at his command, the President, as executive head of the government, and as commander-in-chief of its army and navy, rested neither night nor day, in his preparation for equipment and defence. But at the same time, he linked with preparation for war endeavors toward continued peace.

To the foreign nations who urged him to a peaceful solution of the matter, President McKinley returned a courteous but non-committal answer, declaring to the envoys of the Powers that he shared their hope that peace might be preserved, that the injurious and menacing condition of disturbance in Cuba might be terminated, but adding that, while appreciating "the humanitarian and disinterested character of the communication they had presented on behalf of the Powers," he was still confident that the United States with earnest and unselfish endeavor would fulfil the "duty to humanity by ending a situation the indefinite prolongation of which had become insufferable." All of which was a polite, courteous, and what is called diplomatic way of requesting the Powers of Europe to mind their own business and allow us to take care of our own.

That the condition of affairs in Cuba grew more and more "insufferable" the slow action of the expected "reforms" by Spain amply proved. Madrid promised; but Havana did not perform. The so-called Parliament of Cuba established by Spain for a pretended self-government could neither govern nor stand alone. It was supported by the bayonets of Spain rather than by the will of the Cubans, and death and destruction still wasted the beautiful island.

Then it was that the President of the United States determined no longer to resist the demands of the republic. On the eleventh of April, 1898, he sent a message to Congress in which he reviewed the whole sorry situation of the distressed and fettered island of Cuba and declared that the hour had arrived for America to act.

He explained that the existing rebellion in Cuba was but one in a continuous series of insurrections against Spain which, for more than fifty years, had kept that fair land in disturbance and unrest; which had threatened the security, comfort, commerce, and self-control of the United States, while the barbarities of the present government, like those of its predecessors, had "shocked the sensibilities and offended the humane sympathies" of the American people.

Neutrality, he declared, was ruinous to Cuba's prosperity and expensive to America; this loss and risk had, he said, "so sorely tried the temper and forbearance of our people as to beget a perilous unrest" openly expressed by the people in their newspapers and through their chosen state and national representatives.

His efforts toward friendly mediation and help, he declared, had been refused by Spain. The only result of the existing conflict between Spaniard

THE HOME OF A SUGAR PLANTER.
(On one of the plantations near Santiago.)

and Cuban must, he felt certain, be subjugation or extermination stretched through a long period of years — "a contingency hardly to be contemplated with equanimity by the civilized world," he declared, "and least of all by the United States, affected and injured, deeply and intimately, by its very existence."

If Spain would not give way either to Cuban

revolution or to American mediation; if it were unwise to recognize the belligerent rights or independence of Cuba as a free republic, — as, under the circumstances, did appear most unwise; if, as the destruction of the *Maine* in Havana harbor proved, there was neither safety nor security for an American warship, rightfully sent to Cuban waters on a mission of peace; if, finally, there was no way but one to determine or solve this unbearable problem at our doors, — then, declared President McKinley, that one way must be taken.

What that one way was all men knew, — armed intervention; notice to Spain to quit.

"The long trial," wrote the President to Congress, "has proved that the object for which Spain has waged war cannot be attained. The fire of insurrection may flame or may smoulder with varying seasons, but it has not been and it is plain that it cannot be extinguished by present methods. The only hope of relief and repose from a condition which can no longer be endured is the enforced pacification of Cuba. In the name of humanity, in the name of civilization, in behalf of endangered American interests which give us the right and the duty to speak and to act, the war in Cuba must stop."

These strong and commanding words, deliberately determined upon and calmly proclaimed, found an echo in every true American heart, though the hot-headed still declared that the President had not gone far enough, and the peace-at-any-price people declared he had gone too far. But that "sturdy good sense of the American people," upon which President McKinley always relied, and which can ever be depended upon for decision, justice, and action, again asserted itself, and upheld the President in his firm and final stand.

On the thirteenth of April, Senator Davis of the Committee on Foreign Affairs introduced a report upon the condition of affairs in Cuba and the responsibility of Spain, which closed with a resolution declaring that "the people of Cuba are and of right ought to be free and independent;" that it was the duty of the United States to demand, "and the government of the United States does hereby demand," that Spain relinquish its authority over Cuba and withdraw its forces from the island, and that "the President of the United States be, and hereby is, directed and empowered to use the entire land and naval forces of the United States and to call into the actual service of the United

States the militia of the several States to such an extent as may be necessary to carry these resolutions into effect."

For a week this resolution was debated in Congress by those who wished to uphold and those who wished to forge far ahead of the President. Finally it was passed unanimously by both houses with this significant announcement: " Resolved, that the United States hereby disclaims any disposition or intention to exercise sovereignty, jurisdiction, or control over said island, except for the pacification thereof, and asserts its determination when that is accomplished to leave the government and control of the island to its people."

At noon, on the twentieth of April, President McKinley, in the presence of his Cabinet, signed this joint resolution, and the United States of America was committed to its policy of armed interference in the affairs of Spain and Cuba.

Events followed rapidly. The new Spanish minister at Washington, upon being officially informed of what Congress and the President had decided, at once withdrew from Washington; the Queen Regent of Spain, in presence of the Cortes or Parliament of Spain, called upon " the sons of Spain " to repel this " outrage " by America; the United

States minister at Madrid withdrew from Spain; and this "breaking of diplomatic relations," as it is called, was considered an act of war alike by America and the civilized world; so that war between the United States and Spain is definitely decided to have been actually declared on the twenty-first of April, 1898, when Spain, having refused to accede to the demands of the United States and relinquish its authority in Cuba, withdrew her representative from Washington, dismissed the United States minister from Madrid, and declared her intention to resist and punish the interference of America.

At once, word that war had been virtually declared was telegraphed from Washington to the admiral commanding the United States naval fleet at Key West, and on the twenty-third of April President McKinley issued a proclamation calling for one hundred and twenty-five thousand volunteers to enlist in the war against Spain.

CHAPTER III

HOW THE WAR BEGAN

WAR is a terrible necessity. Some eminent and noble men have denied that it is a necessity and boldly maintained that "there is no such thing as an honorable war or a dishonorable peace." The world's successful fighters have detested it. "War is the trade of barbarians," exclaimed Napoleon, the conqueror of Europe. Washington abhorred it; Lincoln fought against it; and Grant, America's greatest soldier, hated and despised it.

"Let us have peace" was the great general's most famous declaration; but war as a means of peace was his acceptance of the necessity of war.

In this light the war with Spain was a necessity. It became the one and only way of securing the pacification of Cuba, and the ending of those generations of horror and injustice which, for four hundred years, had marked Spain's government in America.

"Occasional war and, therefore, constant preparedness for war," says President Eliot of Harvard, "are still necessary to national security, just as police and courts and prisons are still indispensable to social order and individual freedom in the most civilized and peaceful states." So the republic of the United States declared itself the policeman of America, and set out to arrest and punish the chief disturber of the peace and security of America — Spain in Cuba.

To accomplish this it had an army and navy of unknown possibilities and uncertain strength. Its regular army numbered, as I have told you, somewhat less than twenty-five thousand men; its volunteer militia or national guard, organized by the forty-five states of the Union, amounted to about one hundred and fifteen thousand men, some of them better equipped for war than at any other national crisis, and yet none of them really prepared for actual war. The navy of the United States, remodelled and strengthened during thirty years of peace, had powerful fighting ships and well-drilled seamen, and comprised a fleet of thirty warships large and small, and fifteen thousand marines and sailors. There was also in certain of the states a sort of sea-militia, known as the Naval

HOW THE WAR BEGAN

NEAR MATANZAS.

(A *volante*, or Cuban carriage, the principal vehicle of Matanzas.)

Reserve, of whose ability little was known though much was hoped. This Naval Reserve amounted to less than four thousand men.

But behind regulars, jackies, militia-men, and naval reserves there were fully six millions of American citizens of fighting age, "able to bear arms." To these the President's proclamation came as a summons, and the response to his call for volunteers was immediate and enthusiastic. It was fully ten to one; for over a million of the six available millions expressed their desire to serve in the one hundred and twenty-five thousand required.

Later, an additional call for seventy-five thousand men — "for good measure" — was issued, and, with the increase in the forces of the regular army and navy, a fighting force of over two hundred and seventy-five thousand men answered the call of the President.

It took time and an immense amount of labor to get this fighting force into fighting trim. The navy was ready first. A few additional warships were purchased abroad; picked steamships and yachts were bought, borrowed, or hired at home, and the fighting force of the navy, thanks to the sleepless energy and foresight of the navy department, was increased until it comprised four battle-ships of the first class; one battleship of the second class; two armored cruisers; six coast defence monitors; one armored ram; twelve protected cruisers; three unprotected cruisers; eighteen gunboats; one dynamite cruiser; eleven torpedo boats; vessels of the old navy, including monitors, fourteen. Auxiliary: eleven auxiliary cruisers, twenty-eight converted yachts, twenty-seven converted tugs, fifteen converted colliers, fifteen revenue cutters, seven lighthouse tenders, and nineteen miscellaneous vessels, — one hundred and ninety-five keels of war, fighters or assistant fighters all.

The men enlisting as soldiers in the several states (divided according to the proportionate sizes of their states into what is known as quotas) were attached to certain accepted regiments of the state militia; these, however, were accepted not as state militia, but as regiments of the United States volunteer army sworn into the service of the United States for "two years or the war." These regiments were first mustered in at the state camp grounds of their home state; there they were drilled and disciplined until ready to be transferred to the national camp grounds located in states nearer to the coast or the seat of war — Virginia, Georgia, Alabama, Texas, and Florida — from which camps they were to be despatched as needed for actual service in the field.

War is a costly necessity. To clothe, feed, drill, provide for, and transport this armed force of three hundred thousand men on land and sea, as well as to meet the salary and support of the small army of men and animals that contributed to the success of campaigns, from the high-placed Secretaries of War and the Navy with their assistants, down to the pettiest camp or ship assistant and the smallest burro, demanded an outlay of a fortune a day. Medical officers, hospital helpers and nurses, the thirteen hundred men of the war telegraph and telephone service called the signal corps, with the men of the engineer corps, the secret service men, and the camp and ship helpers, known as non-combatants (teamsters and cooks, scouts and pilots, secretaries, stenographers, messengers and hostlers, firemen, coal passers and transport men),—these and other helpers, high and humble, were necessary to keep the armed forces of the republic in fighting trim afloat and ashore.

The fifty millions of dollars so unanimously placed in the hands of the President by the Congress was speedily used up for the preliminaries of getting ready. More money, and a great deal of it, was needed when war was actually decided upon. National defence was one thing; foreign invasion was another and a much more serious demand.

But Congress was no laggard in this matter. The stamp tax, only resorted to in times of national necessity, was adopted and levied, and a popular loan of money for war expenses was determined upon. By the provisions of this "War Loan Act," the sum of two hundred millions of dollars was asked for from the people, for the use of which the government agreed to pay an annual interest of three per cent. In order that the people might make this loan themselves, and not the rich men and great money corporations, the act declared that no one should be allowed to take more than five thousand dollars of the bonds issued to secure this loan, while those who could only afford to lend the government ten dollars could procure war bonds to that amount.

The result was startling. So great was the people's faith in the strength, resources, and faith of the government that purchasers rushed to buy the bonds; indeed, had the loan been many times larger, it would have been at once taken up; for the subscriptions to the two hundred million dollar war loan were exceeded to five times that amount. The readiness with which Congress and the people supplied the funds needed to carry on the war, besides strengthening the government, gratifying the President, and giving confidence to the nation, had a great effect upon foreign nations; for it was a revelation of the vast resources and internal strength of the United States, and led the nations of the earth to hesitate before giving aid and comfort to enemies of the great republic across the sea. One after another they hastened to declare their neutrality in the war between the United States and Spain; in this they were led on by England, our old-time foe, but now an open friend, bound by ties of race and speech to the republic which so largely sprang from her blood and was now to face in fight that nation with which English war-men had grappled, from the Armada to Trafalgar.

That the days of the Armada and Trafalgar, of Drake and Nelson, were not the days of this generation was shown at the very outset of hostilities, when, in his proclamation of April twenty-six, President McKinley announced to the world that, although not a party to the agreement entered into by European nations forty years ago and known as "the declaration of Paris," the United States would issue no letters of marque and permit no privateering, — that legalized robbery on the high seas. The Spanish government, also not a party to the Paris declaration, promised the same total abstinence from permission to plunder; so, while ships of war were allowed to make prizes of the enemy's merchant ships, at least the brutal privateering, which in all the sea-wars of old had been allowed and legalized, was not practised or permitted. The world, indeed, grows better and more humane as it grows older.

Against the regular and volunteer armies of the United States, and against her ships and seamen, were to be pitted the trained soldiers and the new navy of Spain, two hundred thousand men and one hundred and thirty warships; and though these official figures proved somewhat misleading, they were of sufficient weight to set all the coast towns from Eastport to Galveston and from Seattle to San Diego in a flutter of excitement for fear a Spanish fleet should swoop down upon an extended and unprotected coast-line to ravage and destroy. People, of course, were needlessly disturbed by this "bugaboo" of a Spanish fleet, and I know of more than one simple-minded fisherman on the Maine coast who sent wife and family far into the interior, lest the white house on the headland overlooking the sea should become the victim of Spanish brutality when "them Spaniards" came sailing along the shores, bearing to peaceful homes destruction and death.

The government appreciated this coast-wide fear, and hastened to allay it as far as limited time and actual war needs permitted. Nearly sixteen hundred mines were planted in the larger harbors of the Atlantic and Pacific shores; these, it was believed, would restrain or destroy Spain's marauding fleets; forts were strengthened, batteries planted, and twelve thousand infantry and artillery men were detached for coast defence, while the naval militia of the several states manned the purchased or hired ships of the Auxiliary Navy and patrolled the coast to watch for and give warning of Spanish invasion.

But this never came. Spain's interests were elsewhere. Her work was, throughout the war, defensive rather than offensive, and the superior discipline and seamanship of the American navy permitted no possibility for a descent upon American coast cities for tribute or destruction.

Meantime the army gathered for the invasion of Cuba was being worked into shape. Even the regulars, trained to endure heat and cold, needed to be "acclimated" in the soft southern air of the national camps before they could be transported to the more enervating climate of a Cuban summer, or even that of healthier Porto Rico. This smaller island the government had decided to seize and invade first, as a base of operations against the more formidable Spaniards of Cuba, and as a section better fitted for the massing and feeding of troops than the ravaged and war-stripped island of Cuba.

HOW THE WAR BEGAN

Just how much assistance the struggling patriots of Cuba, with their uncertain, scattered, ill-fed, and poorly disciplined army of guerilla fighters, could give to the soldiers of the United States was an uncertain question. Far off in eastern Cuba, beyond the mountains and in the wasted valley of the Cauto River, once the garden spot of Cuba, lay the patriot general, Calixto Garcia, and his small but brave command. To him, rather than to the hidden and uncertain insurgent Cuban government, the War Department despatched a secret messenger.

A CUBAN SOLDIER.
(Scout, guide, and irregular fighter.)

This was Lieutenant Rowan, a graduate of West Point, and a trustworthy, courageous, and skilful officer. In silence and secrecy, now in an open boat, escaping Spanish watchfulness, now crawling through thickets or riding fifty miles a day over abandoned roads or through the dense Cuban forests, fording rivers, braving the danger of arrest and death as a spy, but all the time safely guided by Cuban scouts, Lieutenant Rowan at last reached the camp of Garcia. Then, with scarcely a half-day's wait between the delivery of his secret despatches and the receipt of his equally secret reply, the brave lieutenant pushed on with his messages across to the northern side of the island, again braving danger and death, and again escaping Spanish vigilance, until at last in an open boat he reached Jamaica and safety, and then Tampa, Washington, and appreciation.

For he had done just what he was detailed to do — located the patriot camp, arranged for the coöperation of Garcia, and brought to the government the reports most desired. For his good work he was complimented by the War Department, made a lieutenant-colonel, and officially thanked by General Miles, the head of the American army, for having performed "an act of heroism and cool daring that has rarely been excelled in the annals of warfare."

Lieutenant Rowan reported to the War Department the result of his mission to Garcia on the eleventh of May. But, before that date, the crisis had passed and delay had burst into action. It was well to delay for the purposes of possible peace or a final preparation; but to the men on the war-

A TYPICAL FARM-HOUSE.
(In the eastern department of Cuba.)

ships rendezvoused off the Florida coast, peace seemed preposterous, and delay was maddening.

In fact, on the very day on which Lieutenant Rowan arrived at Kingston on the island of Jamaica to prepare for his perilous mission, — the twenty-first of April, 1898, — the blue-jackets of Uncle Sam's navy were straining like hounds in leash anxious to spring.

Framed by the blue water and bluer sky, in the coral-reef harbor of Key West, the big warships, in their lead-colored war-paint, swung lazily at their moorings; from the captain commanding to the lowest mess-boy there was fretting at delay, and fear lest things would be so "fixed up" that the new American navy would have no opportunity to show proof of its years of drilling and months of perfected preparations. For Uncle Sam's blue-jackets certainly were spoiling for a fight. They "remembered the *Maine*"; they could not forget their murdered comrades; they believed in the prowess of their warships and the justice of their cause; they knew the might and mettle of the men behind the guns; they burned to put all these to the test and show the republic of what sort of fighting material the white navy (dulled now by its gray war-domino) was made.

So, with fires banked and everything ready for departure, the squadron lay at Key West, waiting; so, going through their daily routine of ship and shore duty, the squadron's officers and men waited and grumbled. Suddenly, on the afternoon of the twenty-second of April, across the wires that stretched from Washington, over the land and under the sea to Key West, flashed the cipher despatch that read when translated: "War is declared; fleet ordered to sea."

That despatch woke the sleepy April air of Key West into instant action. It sent the loiterers on shore hurrying to their ships; it sent the men on shipboard speeding this way and that, all about their big, floating war-homes, from conning-tower to boiler-room, making everything trim and ship-shape; it made Captain Sampson of the great armored cruiser *New York* Admiral Sampson of the blockading squadron; it cast off the mooring-chains of those ships that were ready, it hastened the coaling of those not quite ready, and it sent, at four o'clock on the morning of April twenty-third, the thirteen terrible warships at the Key West rendezvous steaming out to sea, headed for Cuba and for real war at last.

Four days after the shock of real war came. During those four days a few inoffensive and unthinking Spanish merchantmen, ignorant of the declaration of war, hove to as the guns of the warships fired across their bows, and the prize crews of the warships sailed them as prizes into port; these, however, did not really count as war.

But as, on the twenty-seventh of April, the flagship *New York*, the steel cruiser *Cincinnati*, and the monitor *Puritan* drifted off the mouth of the harbor of Matanzas, Cuba's second largest city, fifty-two miles east from Havana, sharp eyes

VIEW FROM THE YUMURI VALLEY, NEAR MATANZAS.
(The Guadeloupe hills. From an etching by Blaney.)

and good glasses on the lookout could see the blue-bloused soldiers of Spain piling up the yellow soil of Matanzas into fortifications against the Yankee invaders.

At once the signals raced from bridge to engine-room; the bugle rang out its melodious call to quarters; officers and blue-jackets, middies and marines, rushed to their proper stations, and Captain Chadwick of the *New York* called out to the boyish ensign who, graduating from the Naval Academy at Annapolis before his full course was completed, was given charge of the big guns "in the waist," amidships, "Aim for four thousand yards; aim for that bank on the point!"

Rip, crash, bang! went the great gun, setting the big warship a-shiver with concussion and vibration; a cloud of smoke swung across the deck; far away on the shore the yellow dirt of the earthworks, stung by the plunging shot, leaped fifty feet in air; the guns of the turrets, fore and aft, thundered out and wreathed the ship in smoke; the *Puritan* and the *Cincinnati*, joining in, opened on the shore batteries that had replied with Spanish shot to Yankee projectile; but the Yankee fire tore the new-flung ramparts, while the Spanish shots spluttered and fell in the water three hundred feet short of damage.

For fifteen minutes the dialogue of fire flashed and roared across the blue water of Matanzas harbor; then, the Spanish batteries were silenced; the signal "cease firing" flew from the flagship; the Yankee warships steamed away, and Ensign Boone, the Annapolis schoolboy, had the proud satisfaction of really opening the war.

CHAPTER IV

HOW ADMIRAL DEWEY SPENT HIS MAY-DAY

ADMIRAL DEWEY.

FAR away across the western ocean, thousands of miles from home, there rode at anchor in various harbors in the early spring days of 1898 a half-dozen warships of the United States navy known as the Asiatic Squadron.

This fleet was under the command of Commodore George Dewey, one of "Farragut's boys" of the old war-days, a cool, clear-headed, and masterful man of the true Farragut sort. His flagship was the second-class steel cruiser *Olympia*, of four eight-inch and five ten-inch guns, which, with the steel cruisers *Baltimore*, *Raleigh*, *Concord*, and *Boston*, the gunboat *Petrel*, and the despatch boat *Hugh McCulloch*, composed the little fleet in Asiatic waters.

Across the China Sea, four hundred miles and more from the Malayan coast, are the Philippine Islands, discovered and occupied for Spain by the famous world-circler Magellan, who named them for Spain's most powerful emperor, Philip the Second, great-grandson of that Ferdinand and Isabella who sent Columbus on his wonderful western voyage.

The Philippine Islands are some twelve hundred in number, of all shapes and sizes, four hundred of them only being inhabited. They are poor in present circumstances, thanks to Spain's selfish rule, but they are rich in possibilities. Upon the largest island, Luzon, stands the capital of the Philippines, Manila, a city of perhaps one hundred and sixty thousand inhabitants — Spain's stronghold on the Pacific. For years, these rich but misgoverned islands had been, like Cuba, in revolt against Spanish rule, now open and destructive, now slumbering and expiring, as Spanish gold rather than Spanish arms subdued the malcontents.

One of these malcontents, an educated Filipino named Emilio Aguinaldo, had gone as a fugitive to Hong Kong. There the enterprising and aggressive representative or consul-general of the United States, Rounsevelle Wildman, had conferred with the refugee, opened correspondence with the equally enterprising assistant secretary of the navy at Washington, Theodore Roosevelt, with the result that, long before war was declared, an understanding was reached by which, if war should come, Commodore Dewey would make a sudden descent upon Manila, the Spanish stronghold.

War was declared, and the watchful Navy Department at once, on April 24, telegraphed to Commodore Dewey, who was collecting his little fleet at Hong Kong: "War has been commenced between the United States and Spain. Proceed at once to the Philippine Islands. Commence operations at once, particularly against Spanish fleet. You must capture vessels or destroy. Use utmost endeavors."

Prompt and efficient in his preparations, Dewey had already been using his "utmost endeavors" to get ready for his trip to the Philippines. He had concentrated his ships, bought two large transports which he loaded with coal and supplies for his fleet, and when, on the twenty-fifth of April, the British governor of Hong Kong, anxious to keep the British assurance of neutrality unbroken, desired the commodore to remove his fleet from neutral waters, Dewey steamed to Mirs Bay, in

ON CORREGIDOR ISLAND.

(At the entrance to the bay and harbor of Manila.)

Chinese territory thirty miles from Hong Kong, and there completed his preparations.

These required scarcely two days for the "finishing touches," and on the afternoon of the twenty-seventh the fleet struck across the China Sea, headed for Luzon and Manila.

It was not so much Manila as the Spanish fleet for which Dewey was headed. The first desire of the Navy Department was to clear the seas of Spanish warships. That accomplished, the fear of Spanish invasion would be removed, and the hands of the government would be free for the one act to which it was pledged, — the forcible expulsion of Spain from the island of Cuba; and that is why Dewey sailed to Manila.

In the landlocked harbor of Manila lay the fleet of the Spanish Admiral Montojo, commanding in Asiatic waters. The Spanish fleet in numbers fully doubled the American fleet. It comprised thirteen in all, — one big steel cruiser, one wooden cruiser, three smaller cruisers, two English-built gunboats, two gun-vessels, one despatch boat, one auxiliary cruiser, and two torpedo boats. Altogether, this fleet had neither the fighting strength nor the superb discipline of Dewey's four fine cruisers, but it lay within the harbor under the protection of the great guns of the well-manned Spanish fortifications, and such a thing as "Yankee success" seemed out of the question.

Indeed, that was the whole tenor of the bombastic proclamation of the Spanish governor-general when he heard that the American fleet had cleared for Manila.

"The struggle," he said, "will be short and decisive. The God of battles will give us one as brilliant as the justice of our cause demands. . . . A squadron manned by foreigners, possessing neither instruction nor discipline, is preparing to come to this archipelago with the ruffianly intention of robbing us of all that means life, honor, and liberty.

"Filipinos! prepare for the struggle; and, united under the glorious Spanish flag, which is ever covered with laurels, let us fight with the conviction that victory will crown our efforts, and to the challenge of our enemies let us oppose, with the decision of the Christian and the patriot, the cry of 'Viva España!'"

That cry appears to be all that the Spanish admiral did prepare to oppose to the American attack. For he seems to have taken few, if any, precautions, save to shelter himself under the guns of the forts which guarded the harbor, and, as every one knows, one gun on shore is considered to be worth four aboard ship.

But when the shore is Spanish, and the ship is American, history now records that what every one knows is not always so. For when, on the evening of April 30, the fleet of Commodore Dewey, with all ports closed, and only one small light on the stern of each ship as a guide to those that followed, arrived off the entrance to Manila Bay, the Spanish scout boats which the commodore supposed would be cruising outside on the watch for the invaders did not put in an appearance. So he steered straight for the gun-crested heights of Corregidor Island, somewhere behind which, he knew, lay the Spanish fleet he had been sent to destroy.

Corregidor is a high and precipitous island, lying one mile off shore and directly in the mouth of the entrance to Manila Bay, which is there about six miles wide. The island rises to a height of six hundred feet, and crowning its crest was a modern battery of big Krupp guns, — the best ship-destroyers in the world. Five miles across on the mainland was the rock-mounted battery of El Fraile, but through the silent night the man who had been schooled by Farragut decided to follow Farragut's tactics and "run the batteries."

Silently, quietly, in single file, the *Olympia* leading, the fleet steamed into the bay, until they were well abreast of the looming height of Corregidor, frowning dimly through the dark. Then a shovelful of soft Japanese coal thrown on the fires of the *McCulloch* set the soot-lined smoke-stack aflame; a rocket, shot up from the Corregidor battery, gave the alarm; the invaders were discovered. But they kept straight on. It was midnight; the ships had all run well into the entrance of the bay, and, save for the signal rocket from Corregidor, no note of their discovery was taken, save as the answering signal lights flashed out along the shore.

Suddenly a big gun from the rock-battery of El Fraile boomed out into the night, and a Spanish shell went screaming over the fleet. The *Raleigh* and the *Concord* gave a quick reply. "Just to tell them we're here," as one of the Yankee gunners said; while the *Boston*, steering straight for El Fraile, opened fire upon the battery, and kept on firing until the Spanish guns were silenced.

The rest of the fleet steamed on, through the darkness of the night, picking their way into a bay and harbor no one on board knew; there was no pilot for the fleet; neither the commodore nor his navigator had ever been in Manila; mines might lay strewn beneath the keels; guns might be trained upon them from the embattled heights or from the encircling shores. But, steering by chart, feeling their way, right forward into the unknown dangers of a blanketing night and a hostile harbor, bow to stern, the *Olympia* leading, the commodore on the bridge, the fleet crept up the channel, unmolested and unstayed, and just as the quick-coming Asiatic dawn came up, as Kipling says, "like thunder 'cross the bay" on the morning of the first of May, the misty outline of the city of Manila came plainly into view.

And there, across the little bay at the head of which lay Cavite with its Spanish arsenals and shipyards, the Spanish fleet rode at anchor, drawn up in battle array, but less prepared for real battle than ever rode a fleet of warships since Antony and Cleopatra lost the world at Actium, and Edward, the third Plantagenet, drowned the French off Sluys. Good ships, good guns, good powder, good equipments, and good men were in that Spanish fleet off Cavite in the Bay of Manila that fateful May-day morning; but Dewey had been too quick for them; they were simply, as the boy or girl at school called upon suddenly to recite an unstudied lesson is forced to answer, "unprepared."

The Yankee commodore and his men, however, could not know this, save as they might suspect it from the absent scout boats and the silent forts. Before them lay the fleet they had been sent to destroy; it was their duty to begin work at once.

They did so. Still sailing in column, Indian file, with the stars and stripes streaming from gaff and masthead, the fleet steered straight for the Spanish line. A shore battery opened fire, but to no effect; and every gun-captain with his crew stood at quarters ready for the signal which they knew must come.

It came speedily. Straight on the *Olympia* steered until within seven thousand yards of the Spanish column; then the signal flashed far below to the engine-room, and, responsive to the touch, the helm swung to port, the bow veered around, and, with every warship following the same motion, stem to stern, the American fleet sailed diagonally broadside past the Spanish ships.

It was half-past five on that brilliant morning of an Asiatic May-day; nearer and nearer drew the Yankee ships, silent, but threatening; at last they were within five thousand yards of the Spanish line of battle; the excitable Don could stand the suspense no longer; and, even as Commodore Dewey, turning to the captain of the *Olympia*, said calmly and quietly, "When you are ready, you may fire, Gridley," the first gun boomed out from the *Reina Christina*, the Spanish flagship, and the battle of Manila Bay had begun.

The two long guns of the *Olympia's* forward turret answered the Spaniard's challenge, and as the smoke wreathed the flagship, every other fighter in the lead-colored Yankee squadron joined in and flung their crashing broadside straight at the Spanish line.

Stung to fury by this attack the Spanish gunners made instant reply; from ship and shore, from turret and gun-deck and battery, came the quick, nervous, aimless shell-shrieks of the "rattled" Spaniards; while, from the arsenal and the city, boats put off, rowing like mad to carry to their respective ships the officers and men of Montojo's squadron, who had been spending the night ashore, never dreaming that the "Yankee pigs" would come so soon or dare so much.

Behind their guns the men of Dewey's squadron

stood to their work in that calm and businesslike manner which is the result of superb discipline. They had faith in their commodore and they were having a chance at "them Spaniards," the chance all sea-fighters crave. The story of their work seems easy as we read it now, but remember where they were and what they had to face. Seven thousand miles from home those six Yankee war-ships had sailed boldly into what, under other circumstances, might well have been a death-trap; confronted by a hostile fleet, encompassed by hostile shores, ringed about with hostile batteries and forts, they had nevertheless "taken the initiative," and sailed straight for victory or ruin; there was no alternative; they had simply "got to win"; every man, from the commodore on the bridge to the stoker at the blazing furnace, knew this, and proceeded to do, each man, his "level best."

Now mark the difference between "getting rattled" and "keeping cool." For two hours seventy Spanish guns on ship and shore were hurling their deadly projectiles at a fleet of six unprotected cruisers within easy range, and but one of their shells wounded a man or did any damage to the American ships; within that same space of time the American warships, steaming slowly five times

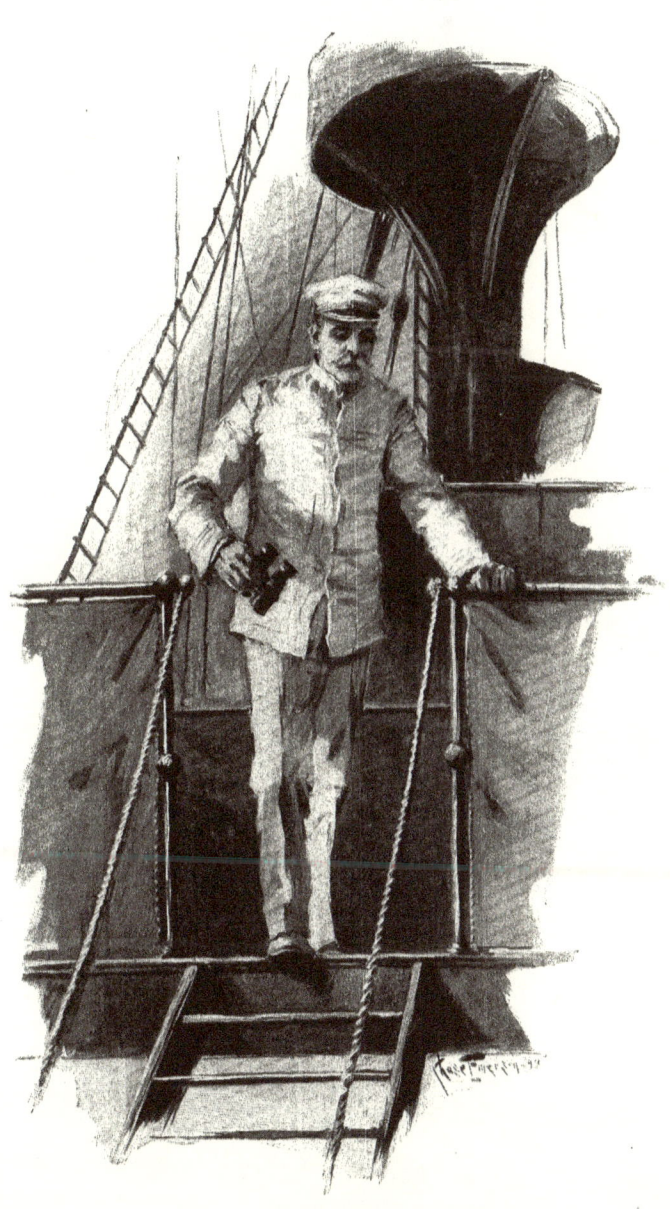

DEWEY AT MANILA.

("When you are ready, Gridley, you may begin.")

HOW ADMIRAL DEWEY SPENT HIS MAY-DAY

before the Spanish column and manned by blue-jackets who for twenty-four hours had been held in readiness without sleep or rest, keyed up to the excitement of a foreseen battle, sent such a storm of well-directed shots at the Spanish fleet, as to set the Spaniards' flagship ablaze, utterly silence the guns of the big wooden cruiser, and put all the others out of the fight.

Advancing, turning, and advancing again, now the port and now the starboard batteries of Dewey's fleet were constantly in play; even as they circled about for one of these terrific broadsides, two mines, sunken for secret assassination, exploded just ahead of the *Olympia's* bow, while two torpedo boats, dashing out from the Spanish column, sought to blow up the ship with their deadly missiles. But Dewey was ready for them. The mines exploded too far in advance to do any damage, and as for the two torpedo boats, as the commodore said in his very modest report of the battle, "One was sunk, and the other, disabled by our fire, was beached before they were able to fire their torpedoes."

Then the beautiful *Reina Christina*, the flagship of the Spanish admiral, fired with a desperate resolve, boldly dashed out of the battle line and headed straight for the *Olympia*, to engage at short range and meet and overwhelm the American flagship "rail to rail." It was a brave challenge; but the commodore was prepared — as he always was.

"Even before she could reach us," says Dewey's report, "she was received with such a galling fire — the entire battery of the *Olympia* being concentrated upon her — that she was barely able to return to the shelter of the point."

It was indeed a "galling fire" with which the Yankee flagship greeted the Spanish admiral. As if to support the attack of their flagship, the whole fire of the Spanish fleet was turned upon the *Olympia;* but the guns of the American squadron followed suit on their side, and when the *Reina Christina* attempted to stem that terrible fire of "bursting steel," it swept her, crippled her, and drove her back. "Her sides crushed in, her men melted away," says one account; and, even as she turned to flee, the eight-inch gun of the *Olympia's* forward turret sent a shell hurtling toward her that raked the Spanish flagship from stem to stern, killing and wounding her captain and sixty men and sending her drifting back to cover, "a flaming wreck from which every man, able to do so, was fleeing for life."

It had been a gallant effort, — that dash to death, — for which the Spanish admiral deserves all praise as a brave sea-fighter, but scarcely as an able seaman; no one ship, or any dozen, indeed, that floated the Spanish flag could stem that terribly destroying fire that came from the ready guns of the American fleet.

Five times, as I have said, did Dewey's fleet pass and repass the Spanish line. And when the fifth run was made, every Spanish ship was either disabled or on fire; the shore batteries before Manila were silenced by the threat of the commodore that unless they ceased firing he would train his guns on the town; then, as the day was growing hot and the temperature in the magazines and the boiler-rooms was crawling up well toward the "sizzling point" of one hundred and fifty degrees, the commodore, as he reports, "at twenty-five minutes to eight ceased firing and withdrew the squadron for breakfast."

That was the report that thrilled all America when the tidings of Dewey's great May-day fight reached his home-land. But we know now that while, ostensibly, the commodore drew off for "breakfast," he was really himself in a serious frame of mind. Unharmed and victorious, indeed, his ships were; but that continual and destructive bombarding had drawn so deeply upon his store of ammunition that it was a question how much longer the attack could be kept up. Then, too, the commodore and his officers did not yet appreciate the real ruin their fire had worked upon the Spanish fleet. Smoke and flame they saw; but the enemy still held their battle-line, and if they possessed the pluck and ability to hold out, what resource had this daring American fleet, cooped up in a hostile harbor within range of hostile batteries and a stubborn fleet? Still the jackies on the warships felt certain that their victory was complete and even grudged the call to breakfast.

"Let's keep at it and finish 'em up," they demanded. The "finish" came soon, and the ammunition held out to the end.

"About half-past eight," wrote home one of the assistant engineers on the *Olympia*, "the whole fleet took a rest and something to eat. At twenty minutes to eleven we went for them again to finish them up."

This proved, after all, to be the easiest part of the day's work, in spite of the commodore's apprehensions. It was cruel, — but when was war ever other than cruel? And it was necessary, you see, because the Spaniards had not yet cried, "Hold! enough!"

They did so speedily. The burning and disabled hulks had been moved, by order of the admiral, nearer in shore, and when at twenty minutes to one, the little gunboat *Petrel* steamed up into the creek and shelled the fleet and the arsenal, the guns of the *Baltimore* raked the wrecks off Cavite and dismounted three guns on the Spanish fort; then the yellow flag of Spain came down from its staff on the arsenal; the white flag of surrender fluttered in its place; the signal "cease firing" flew from the *Olympia*, and, at half-past twelve, "the Spanish batteries being silenced and the ships sunk, burned, and deserted," so ran the commodore's report, "the squadron returned and anchored off Manila." Commodore Dewey had kept his May-day in glorious, sea-fighting fashion, the battle of Manila Bay was over, and Spain had lost her fleet in Asiatic waters.

Then the squadron drew away from the shattered hulks and occupied a mooring-ground under the very guns of Manila, overawed into silence.

The heavy air of the Orient rang with the cheers of Yankee blue-jackets over the signal victory won by Yankee pluck and daring and discipline. The men were proud of their commodore, the commodore was proud of his men, and all were proud of their victorious ships. From the stately flagship down to the little *Petrel*, "the baby battleship," as the jackies called her for her valiant work at Cavite, every one had done royal service.

Then the *McCulloch* steamed swiftly to Hong Kong. The news of victory flashed beneath the wide ocean, and soon the whole world knew how Commodore George Dewey, U.S.N., spent his May-day in the year 1898. A shout of pride and joy went over the land from Maine to Georgia and from Massachusetts Bay to the Golden Gate. Dewey had done his duty, obeyed orders, and placed his name high on his country's roll of heroes as the victor in one of the most brilliant and one of the most astounding naval victories in all history.

He had been ordered to find and destroy the Spanish fleet. This he had accomplished, as the advertisements say, "with neatness and despatch." Spain's Asiatic fleet was annihilated; Spain's Asiatic colonies were wrested from Spain.

For good or for evil this was the result. For, though timid and hesitating Americans there are who say that when the commodore had performed his mission and wrecked the ships of Spain he should have sailed away, all men know that this he could not do. The boom of Dewey's resistless guns had opened a new chapter in American history, and propounded a problem that America herself must solve, — the question of her rights of possession, and the wisdom of occupation in lands far away from the domain of the republic.

Spain had lost, but her men had fought valiantly. The smoking hulks of her ruined battleships were the graves of many brave and fearless men, — brave, if lacking in marksmanship, fearless, if wanting in discipline. "They died game," one American sailor declared, and this verdict was the verdict of the fleet. From the Admiral Montojo, who, when his flagship broke into flames, hauled down his pennant, and, like Perry on Lake Erie, rowed off to raise it on another ship, down to the humblest seaman and stoker, the Spanish sailors fought a losing fight; but they battled manfully and died by the hundreds for the honor of Spain.

Four hundred men in killed and wounded marked the death-record for Spain; that of the Americans was not a single life lost, not a single boat disabled, and but eight men wounded by flying splinters.

So ended the first sea-fight of the new American navy; the first, too, in which American warships and sailors had been engaged for over a generation. It was a victory of discipline over incompetency, of confidence over uncertainty, of preparedness over procrastination, of the Yankee "ready" over the Spanish "*manana*."

It carried many poor fellows down to death, innocent of harm, but the instruments of an inhuman power; it awoke ringing applause and hero-worship in every American heart, but it brought directly to American consideration an unexpected, unsought, and perplexing problem.

For this problem, however, Americans themselves were largely responsible; their navy was efficient in action, superb in drill, perfect in discipline; it worked like the well-adjusted and well-oiled parts of a splendid machine. But the machine was not large enough; the size of the navy was not equal to its efficiency; the world, because of that navy's numerical weakness, had never appreciated its inherent strength.

The Philippine problem forced upon the American people by Commodore Dewey is, as I have said, due, itself, largely to the American people themselves; or, as Captain Mahan, the ablest living student of sea-power and its results, declares, had there been ample coast defences along our shores and a navy half as large again as the white squadron of 1897, the world would have been enlightened and Spain would have chosen the easier part of discretion. "Our evident naval supremacy," says Captain Mahan, "would have kept the Spanish fleet in Europe; there would have been no war, and, thanks to a great and prosperous navy, there would have been no question of the Philippines and, possibly, none of Hawaii."

As to that, no man can be sure; for events move quite otherwise, sometimes, from the course men would give them. But as to Commodore Dewey's victory in Manila Bay in the morning flush of an Asiatic May-day, even with all its destruction and all its terrible war-fruits, the republic will ever assert with Southey's old peasant of Blenheim: —

"Why, that I cannot tell," said he;
"But 'twas a glorious victory."

CHAPTER V

WHY THE UNITED STATES NAVY PLAYED AT HIDE-AND-SEEK

REAR-ADMIRAL SAMPSON.

WHILE Dewey and his men were scoring the first fighting success of the war on the distant Malayan coast, their countrymen at home were by no means idle. The land forces were mustering rapidly. From distant posts and frontier forts the regular army, increased to full fighting strength, was moving toward the southern coast; in temporary state camps the volunteers were being drilled into shape; while, one by one, their regiments, as they attained proficiency, were transported to the national encampments, where, on the historic field of Chickamauga, amid the sands of Tampa, and at other hastily selected sites in the south, regulars and volunteers awaited the command "On to Cuba!"

But that command lagged in its coming — too much so, certain of the over-confident soldier-boys and far too many thoughtless newspapers and people declared. For the mobilizing and disciplining of an army of two hundred thousand volunteer fighters, the most of whom had never seen war and to very many of whom a gun and a uniform were as unfamiliar as a "gentleman-sportsman's hunting-kit," were things that called for patience, consideration, and much necessary delay.

More than this, however: even where a fair proportion of the army of invasion was ready to move, the risk of transfer could not at once be taken.

Spain was known to have certain fleets of war-ships which, on paper at least, and according to all reports, were sufficiently formidable to be avoided. One shot from an eight-inch gun in a forward turret or from a sneaking torpedo boat could crush and sink the stoutest unprotected transport crowded with soldiers, horses, and munitions of war. For these transports, which were to convey the American army across the water to Cuba, were steamships rented to the government at so much a day or purchased for this especial work from the merchant marine — good steamers, most of them, but none of them prepared to meet a warship in fight or even to run away from one of those destroying sea-monsters urged on in pursuit by the extra exertion of "forced draught." Delay in moving troops was preferable to the possible loss of brave soldiers sunk by a shot from a warship or by the horrible missiles sent out from the torpedo tubes.

THE TRANSPORTS EN ROUTE TO CUBA.

But what about our warships? you may ask; were they not designed and manned for attack and defence? were they not strong enough to convoy and protect our fleets of transports and prevent or repel the sudden onset of Spanish destroyers?

AT HIDE-AND-SEEK

That certainly was one of the duties which devolved upon our fierce fighting squadron. But there were other duties, too. I have told you of our vast unprotected coast-line, and of the fears of the inhabitants of our crowded and wealthy coast cities lest a sudden onset of an unknown Spanish fleet, swooping down upon them, should visit upon them ruin, destruction, and death. The people of the inland cities and towns were inclined to "poke fun" at the perturbed dwellers by the sea for their fears and fright; but, all the same, those fears and frights were as excusable and justifiable in 1898 as they had been in the trying days of 1798 and 1812, when the fear of foreign war terrified the Atlantic coast and put its people in jeopardy.

At all events, the government was forced to recognize this pardonable fear; therefore, to allay it, they established an armed patrol of scouts and warships, which hovered about the coast or ran into the larger seaports, so that, from Savannah to Bar Harbor, the people might feel that the safety of their lives and property was being cared for by the national government.

One other duty the navy had laid upon it. It must intercept, locate, bottle up, or destroy the fleet or fleets of Spain.

Just how many of these there were the government was not absolutely certain, although its spies and "secret service agents" were wide awake and vigilant. The people, less well informed, decreased or magnified the floating force of the enemy, according as security or fear controlled their statements.

Looking back now, with the facts all known, it is easy to say, as it is to see, that these fears were needless; but what is called the "point of view" depends upon circumstances, and what we know to-day we did not know yesterday. Even though elaborate statements and comparisons were made, giving in parallel columns the strength of the rival fleets of Spain and the United States, there was always the awful chance that those parallels might not be reliable, and that, all unknown to our government, Spain might have a strong auxiliary fleet or certain new, unknown, and powerful warships secreted to hurl at us when and where least expected.

So it became necessary to watch for and intercept any and all Spanish fleets that might be afloat, before they could coöperate with the Spanish troops in Cuba or work destruction upon the coasts of the United States. Dewey did this brilliantly and effectively in Manila Bay. One Spanish fleet, which the Pacific coast feared, was, on that glorious first of May, removed forever from the seas; it now remained for the warships on the Atlantic coast to be equally vigilant and equally effective.

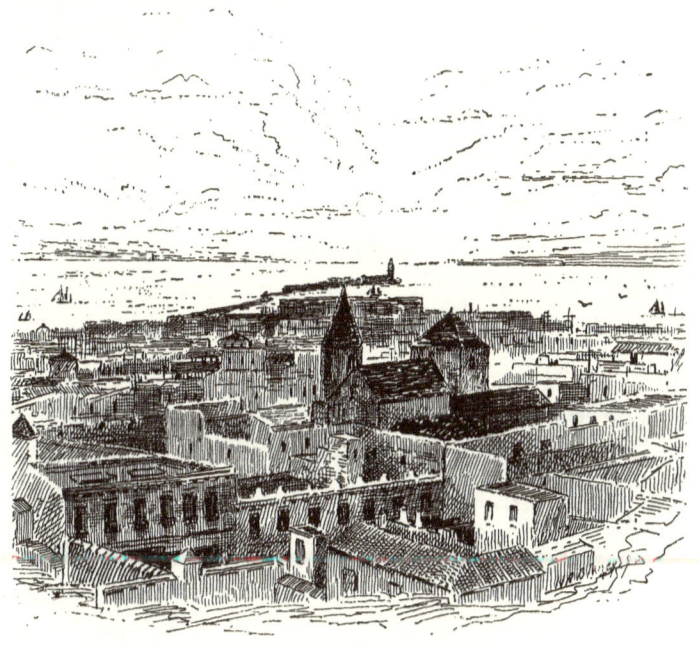

THE CITY OF CADIZ, IN SPAIN.
(From this port sailed Cervera's fleet.)

Spurred on by the achievement of their brothers on the other side of the world, the Atlantic fleets kept vigilant watch and ward, and when it was learned that, on the twenty-ninth of April, Admiral Cervera with a fleet of Spanish cruisers and torpedo boats, sailing first from the home port of Cadiz, had left the rendezvous at the Cape Verde Islands and was heading across the Atlantic, the navy's business of blockading Cuba, convoying transports, capturing merchant prizes, and heading off unlocated Spanish fleets became a most absorbing and sometimes a most perplexing combination of duties.

In fact, there began in the early days of May a regular game of hide-and-seek, in which the United States navy was "it," and went searching about, from Nova Scotia to Venezuela, for the sly Spanish hiders, who wouldn't even cry "coop!"

The game was started when, on the eighth of May, the Secretary of the Navy at Washington telegraphed the admiral of the fleet, off the coast of Hayti, "Do not risk or cripple your vessels against fortifications, so as to prevent soon afterward successfully fighting Spanish fleet composed of *Pelayo*, *Carlos V.*, *Oquendo*, *Vizcaya*, *Maria Teresa*, *Cristobal Colon*, and four deep-sea torpedo boats, if they should appear on this side."

It was a wise order, for it strengthened the determination of Admiral Sampson to withstand, even as he had already withstood, the pleas of his officers for "just one shot," and to waste neither powder nor life unnecessarily. Since the bombardment of the fortifications at Matanzas on April 27, and the silencing of the forts at Port Cabanas, two days later, the blockading fleet had done little more than blockade ports and cut ocean cables.

This cable-cutting was an important act of war, for it broke the Spanish communication with Cuba, and to effect it, the men of the fleet were ready to risk much. The cable connecting Havana and Key West had first been cut, and the three others, which, by different sea-routes, led from the island to Jamaica and Hayti, were next attacked. Near Cienfuegos, on the south coast of Cuba, on the eleventh of May, while attempting to sever one of these cables, the cutters in their row-boats and steam launches, although "covered" by a cruiser and a gunboat, were attacked by Spanish soldiers, a thousand strong. Under a withering fire from the shore, scarcely a hundred feet away, the men at the oars and the men at the cables worked on for two hours grimly unmindful of the whistling shot, and at last the cable was cut, at an expense of two men killed and seven wounded.

That same day, the eleventh of May, while attempting to lure out of their hiding-place in the harbor of Cardenas three Spanish gunboats, the torpedo boat *Winslow*, never designed for such purpose, dashed into the harbor in company with the gunboat *Wilmington* and the revenue cutter *Hudson*. Pushing straight for the docks around which the Spanish gunboats were hidden, the *Winslow* ran into a trap of gunboats and shore batteries; but she pluckily held her own, the *Hudson* supporting her, until the hot Spanish fire crippled her steering gear. In response to a signal the little revenue cutter steamed in to tow the *Winslow* out; but, just as the tow-line was thrown, a Spanish shell fell on the gunboat's deck, killing four of the *Winslow's* men and wounding three.

Among the killed was young Ensign Bagley, who was superintending the withdrawal of the *Winslow* — the first officer to be killed in the war with Spain. Two batteries and two of the Spanish gunboats had been silenced by the attack; but the record of injury and death of that eleventh of May at Cienfuegos and Cardenas, though comparatively small, was the highest total of loss in naval engagements through the entire war. For this, the inefficiency of Spanish marksmanship was to be thanked, not

AT HIDE-AND-SEEK

the cautiousness of Yankee blue-jackets; they courted danger rather than avoided it, and had the standard of Spanish marksmanship been high, the American death-roll in the war with Spain might have been appalling.

But these feats of cable-cutting and harbor-dashing were simply episodes in the story of blockade and watchfulness. The main thing for that blockading fleet to do was to locate or engage Spain's fighting squadron, which was somewhere out on the Atlantic.

Just where that "somewhere" was proved the mystery that kept the navy department "guessing," and sent the warships dodging, now this way and now that, seeking the hiders and trying to catch them before they could "touch goal."

It was known that, beside Cervera's fleet, there was another collecting under the command of Admiral Camara, and how soon these would be ready for service could not be definitely known. So, with one fleet ranging about the Atlantic and another preparing to follow, the defence of the Atlantic coast and the efficient blockade of Cuba called for all the vigilance and watchfulness that the department and the navy combined could give.

A detachment of cruisers was stationed in Hampton Roads, under command of Commodore Winfield Scott Schley. It was known as the Flying Squadron, and it was to be in readiness to dash out, north or south, upon sudden orders, and "tackle" the Spanish fleet wherever it should appear. It thus had the double duty of protecting the Atlantic coast or joining the blockading fleet if its help were needed. The monitors were stationed at Key West, the nearest point to Havana, in case they were needed there, while Admiral Sampson's fleet divided its time between patrolling the West Indian lines around Cuba and Porto Rico, or from there to Key West, endeavoring all the time to keep in direct communication with the Navy Department, which, in Washington, was struggling to play "I spy" and locate Cervera's fleet.

These struggles kept attention racing all over the map of the Atlantic. The air was full of rumors and reports. May 6, the Spanish fleet was reported at Guadeloupe; the same day it was located at St. Thomas; May 8, it was divided between the home harbor of Cadiz in Spain and Diamond Rock, off the island of Martinique; May 9, an outlook on a mountain top had seen it steaming past Cape Haitien; and that same day it was reported as heading for the harbor of San Juan, in Porto Rico. As

AT HIDE-AND-SEEK 101

this seemed plausible, Admiral Sampson dashed away with some of his big ships to San Juan, where he arrived on the morning of the twelfth of May.

THE DIAMOND ROCK, OFF MARTINIQUE.
(As seen through the port-hole of a cruiser.)

Meantime a valuable addition to the Atlantic fleet was racing around the world to be in at the end of the game. This was the powerful battleship *Oregon*, — a veritable floating fortress with sixteen great guns and a speed of seventeen knots an hour.

On March 19, this "bull-dog of the American navy," as the *Oregon* has been called, sailed under "hurry orders" from her berth in San Francisco, where she had been brought down from Puget Sound, to join the squadron at Key West "in case she might be needed," — for on the nineteenth of March, war, though not yet declared, seemed unavoidable.

It was a race against time. With full coal bunkers and all her drafts going, she steamed out of the Golden Gate at eight o'clock on the morning of March 19, and in sixteen days ran into Callao to recoal and clean up the machinery. She had made the run of four thousand miles in two days less than the time made by the regular mail steamer. After a three days' stop the *Oregon*, fully recoaled, sailed from Callao, on Tuesday, April 7, with the air as thick with rumors of hostile Spanish warships as it was of fog, and in nine days more she ran into the Straits of Magellan; the next night she dropped anchor at the Chilian coaling-station of Sandy Point. Here she again recoaled and had her machinery inspected, and at sunrise on Tuesday, April 21, steamed out of the strait, keeping a sharp lookout for a Spanish torpedo boat which, it was rumored, was lying in wait for the big warship in the narrow strait. But the dreaded torpedo boat did not put in an appearance, and swinging out into the Atlantic, the *Oregon* turned her great prow northward to join the fighting fleet.

Whether there was to be any fighting for that fleet or for her own five hundred men, the *Oregon* did not know as she ploughed the Atlantic billows; but when, on the thirteenth of April, the *Oregon* steamed into the harbor of Rio de Janeiro, her men heard that war had been declared; and on the fourth of May, when, with refilled coal bunkers and with her machinery in good trim, she sailed out of Rio harbor, her men had heard of Dewey's great work at Manila, and burned to find equal opportunity for action in Cuban waters. In token of which every blue-jacket bought at Rio a red ribbon stamped " Remember the *Maine*," and wore it on the funny round cap which is the incomprehensible top-piece of a sailor's toggery. And not to be behindhand in open faith in his big warship, Captain Clark of the *Oregon* telegraphed, so it is said, this plea to the Navy Department: " Please don't tangle me up with instructions. I am not afraid of the whole Spanish fleet."

She was, apparently, to encounter nothing but Spanish rumors, but these were plentiful enough. On May 8, the *Oregon* was at Bahia; there she put on her lead-colored war-paint and steamed away next day for Barbadoes, where, after sixteen hours of coaling, she headed for the Florida coast, and on the twenty-fourth of May, after signalling her arrival off Jupiter Light, awaited orders from Washington.

Those orders sent her to Key West to await instructions. Thither she steamed, and on Thursday, the twenty-sixth of May, she dropped anchor off Sandy Key Light — victor in a race against time, fifteen thousand miles in two months and one week, the longest and swiftest voyage ever made by a ponderous battleship.

That she was a victor was due to her superb construction, the masterly way in which she was handled at sea, and the devotion and spirit of her men. From captain to apprentice-boy every man and boy of the five hundred was bound to make a record. And they did. Nights of sleepless vigil, days of double duty, deeds of daring (like that of the boiler-maker who crawled over the banked coal of the furnace to repair a leak around a socket bolt), terrific heat below deck, restless watchfulness above, and then, after fifty-nine days at sea — " through two oceans and three zones," vigilant against a hidden enemy no less than a treacherous sea, to swing into port without a delay or a

THE HARBOR OF SAN JUAN IN PORTO RICO.
(Where Admiral Sampson hoped to find Cervera.)

mishap — "All in good health; everything shipshape; no accidents; not even a hot journal" came the report from Key West — this was a triumph of American shipbuilders, American seamen, American engineers, and American pluck, of which all America might well be proud — as it was!

On the very day on which the *Oregon* was forging ahead between Bahia and Barbadoes, Admiral

Sampson with his nine warships appeared off the port of San Juan on the north coast of Porto Rico, where he hoped to find those artful dodgers — the Spanish fleet.

They were not there; but the Spanish batteries were. So, after an artillery duel of nearly three hours, in which two warships were struck, two men killed, and the Spanish batteries severely "punished,"—damaged, but not destroyed,—the admiral concluded that the Spanish needle was not to be found in the San Juan haystack, and steamed back to Havana.

With the army not ready to move, and the navy so divided in the search for the Spanish fleet that ships and men could not be spared to hold San Juan even if it were captured, the admiral's decision was wise. San Juan was simply "punished," and the hunt for Cervera went back again to Cuba.

But on his way back to Havana, Admiral Sampson was boarded by a press-boat from St. Thomas reporting that the Spanish fleet had gone back to Spain. At once he telegraphed the Navy Department for the truth, and also asked that a collier be sent to San Juan; for, if Cervera had turned back for Cadiz, then he, Sampson, would himself turn back and reduce San Juan.

AT HIDE-AND-SEEK

But the despatch boat sent to Cape Haitien with the admiral's telegrams returned with the information that seven Spanish warships were coaling, or waiting to coal, at Curaçoa; then came other despatches saying they were bound either for Venezuela or Martinique.

At once Admiral Sampson made up his mind. If the Spanish fleet were really at Curaçoa, its destination, he believed, was not Havana, but some nearer port, probably on the south side of Cuba; for

THE NEW YORK.
(Flagship of Admiral Sampson of the blockading fleet.)

Curaçoa, you know, is south of Cuba, off the mouth of the Orinoco. So the admiral set his scouts and auxiliary cruisers scouring the West Indian waters; and to one of his captains, on the fifteenth of May, he cabled, "Destination of Spanish fleet now at Curaçoa probably Santiago de Cuba or San Juan, Porto Rico." And Santiago, as you now know, is the chief city on the south side of Cuba. The game of hide-and-seek was rapidly nearing the end.

But though Admiral Sampson felt confident that he was on the right track, the Navy Department was not so sure. Monitors, despatch boats, and scouts were sent speeding this way and that; the Flying Squadron, under command of Commodore Schley, was ordered to Cienfuegos, and one of the scouting cruisers was hurried off to Venezuela Gulf, where it was thought the Spanish fleet was bound. The admiral himself was ordered to Key West, from which port, after coaling, he was sent with a formidable fleet back to the Havana blockade.

And behold! on the very morning that Schley and his Flying Squadron sailed away from Key West for Cienfuegos, while telegrams were speeding to Washington from consuls and ministers along the Caribbean that "Spanish men-of-war" were here, there, and everywhere, just after one of the scouting cruisers had cut some cables and left Santiago harbor, and Sampson with his peripatetic fleet was coaling at Key West, the Spanish admiral, Cervera, calmly led his fleet into the narrow harbor of Santiago and anchored it in front of the city, still

AT HIDE-AND-SEEK

hidden from the seeking squadron of the American navy. So far the Spaniards had had the best of the game.

But Sampson, though willing to try Cienfuegos, was certain that Santiago was the Spanish hiding-place. So, while keeping a strict blockade of Cienfuegos by Commodore Schley, he sent a scout to Santiago, and next day directed Schley himself to "proceed with all despatch, but cautiously, to Santiago de Cuba, and if the enemy is there, blockade him in port."

But Commodore Schley had ideas of his own. He had seen so much smoke in the harbor of Cienfuegos that he felt certain the Spanish fleet was hiding there, and not at Santiago. The lights of a fleet had been seen at night far to the south of Santiago, and, as the commodore himself had heard guns firing as he approached Cienfuegos, he was certain he had run the game to cover. "I think I have them here almost to a certainty," he wrote the admiral from his station at Cienfuegos.

Admiral Sampson, however, was firm in his opinion, — so firm, in fact, that he repeated his order for Schley to go to Santiago. So to Santiago the commodore sailed, and at seven in the evening on the twenty-ninth of May he was able to hurry off this despatch to the admiral: "Enemy in port. Recognized *Cristobal Colon* and *Infanta Maria Teresa* and two torpedo boats moored inside Morro, behind point. Doubtless others are here. We are short of coal."

So the game was over, and the hider was "spied." Six American warships blockaded the port of Santiago within whose tortuous harbor the Spaniards swung at bay, and the wise judgment of the commanding admiral was fully established. It only remained for him now to catch the expert dodgers who had given four thousand miles of seacoast a terrible fright and kept the Yankee warships racing all over the West Indian waters on a mighty game of hide-and-seek.

CHAPTER VI

HOW THEY BOTTLED UP THE SPANISH FLEET AT SANTIAGO

LIEUTENANT HOBSON.

COMMODORE SCHLEY was a well-satisfied man, even if things had turned out otherwise than he anticipated. He had "located" the Spanish fleet, and as, with the *Brooklyn* leading, his Flying Squadron ran close in to the harbor at Santiago, and then swept across it so that every man on the lookout could actually see the cornered ships of Spain, the commodore, on the bridge of the *Brooklyn*, nodded approvingly and said, "There they are, sure enough. Well, they'll be a long time getting home."

Ill-fated ships of Spain! Their home, to-day, is beneath the surf and sand of the fatal coast of Cuba or beside the grinding coral reefs of historic

Guanahani. For them, came never again the pride and pomp of a gallant entrance into Cadiz harbor, with Spain's golden standard floating from masthead and gaff. Their doom was sealed when they slipped stealthily in through the narrow neck of the Santiago bottle, which now only needed corking up to hold it sealed securely.

As Schley's squadron sailed across the entrance to the harbor, like so many detectives at police headquarters, "identifying" the entrapped Spaniards, all doubt was removed. "Right across the entrance, but inside the Morro batteries," says one report, "lay the *Colon*, her white awnings glistening in contrast with her black hull, easily distinguishable by her peculiar rig of military mast between smokestacks; a little farther in lay another cruiser, one of the *Vizcaya* class." The other boats of the Spanish squadron swung at their moorings, stretching up the bay; but neither from ship nor shore came the bombarding protest against the American intrusion, and, having thus satisfied himself, the commodore steamed out to sea again, and strung his blockaders about the entrance to the harbor; there the fleet, increased soon after by the arrival of the admiral and his ships, held on relentlessly until the final tragedy.

BOTTLING UP THE FLEET AT SANTIAGO 113

Admiral Sampson, who, from the first, had believed Santiago to be the hiding-place of Cervera's fleet, knew the shore line of that harbor well, and believed that it was possible so to block up the narrow entrance as to render escape impos-

IN THE HARBOR OF SANTIAGO.
(Where Cervera's fleet ran in to hide.)

sible, and thus relieve the blockading squadron of a goodly share of its burdensome duties.

He determined to attempt this by placing a condemned or unsatisfactory warship directly across the narrow ship-channel in the entrance to Santiago harbor; there he would deliberately scuttle her, so that she would sink quickly and thus effectually close the harbor to the entrance or exit of warships. The idea was neither new nor novel, but it was highly practical, and, for the task, could it be attempted, the admiral selected the collier *Merrimac*.

In pursuance of this plan, on the twenty-seventh of May, he wrote to Commodore Schley, who was just then preparing to go to Santiago, to remain there on the blockade "at all hazards" and to use the collier *Merrimac* to "obstruct the channel at its narrowest part leading into the harbor. . . . I believe that it would be perfectly practicable," said the admiral, "to steam the vessel into position and drop all her anchors, allow her to swing across the channel, then sink her, either by opening the valves or whatever means may seem best."

Just what were the best means the admiral, at that moment, could not say; but there was, just then, on the admiral's flagship *New York*, as she lay coaling at Key West, a young officer named Richmond Pearson Hobson. He was what is called an assistant naval constructor — that is, one schooled in the construction, strength, and working qualities of vessels and who knew just how a warship was built from keel to fighting top, just where lay its greatest weakness and just where its

BOTTLING UP THE FLEET AT SANTIAGO

chief strength. In fact, it was to study the strength and weakness of the vessels in the admiral's fleet that Mr. Hobson had been detailed for inspection duty on the squadron — especially with a view to deciding which ships could best bear their part on the firing line and which were least able to face attack by torpedo boat or sunken mine.

Assistant Naval Constructor Hobson had been with Sampson during the San Juan bombardment, when he had begged the privilege of running into the harbor at midnight on a steam launch to sweep away mines, locate sunken vessels, and prepare the way for the cruisers to go safely in; but the admiral, as you know, had but one object in view then, — to locate the wandering Spanish fleet, — and he could not afford to risk a single vessel or a single man in such an attempt.

Then Hobson devised a plan for forcing the harbor of Havana with unsinkable and indestructible boats of a peculiar pattern; but when he proposed the plan to Sampson, the admiral said it was not so much unsinkable as sinkable vessels that bothered him, and he asked Mr. Hobson if he saw any way to safely scuttle and sink a collier across the channel in Santiago harbor and thus securely "bottle up" Cervera.

"Confidentially, Mr. Hobson," said the admiral, "I may say to you that we start for Santiago at once, and that I have suggested to Commodore Schley that he scuttle and sink the collier *Merrimac* in the mouth of Santiago harbor. I want to hurry down there to see that it is done; but how to do it swiftly and surely, is a problem. Have you anything to suggest?"

Hobson brought all his intelligence and experience to bear upon the problem, and after thinking it over for some time, he declared that it could be done either by driving off the iron bottom plates from the inside of the ship, or by blowing them up from the outside by well-placed torpedoes.

"I believe it could be done, sir," said the assistant naval constructor, as he and the admiral together studied the chart of Santiago harbor; "and with your permission," he added, "I should like to undertake the work. I am certain I could sink the *Merrimac* at just the right point."

"We'll think it over, Mr. Hobson," replied the admiral, pleased with the young man's enthusiasm. "Take time for the problem; study the question in detail, and report to me. We get under way to-night."

Next day the *New York* and the *Oregon* were

BOTTLING UP THE FLEET AT SANTIAGO

racing along toward Santiago, and the assistant naval constructor was laying before the admiral his well-conceived plan for sinking the *Merrimac*. The admiral grew more and more interested and was soon studying, with Hobson, the best plan for running the big collier past the shore batteries and getting her to the desired spot unharmed.

It sounds very simple. All that was required was to sail the condemned collier into the harbor, lay her across the channel, blow a hole in her, and let her sink right across the channel where she had been laid. But who was to do all this? How could she run the Spanish batteries? What would become of the brave men who took her in?

"Few realize," says Captain Mahan, "the doubts, uncertainties, and difficulties of the sustained watchfulness which attends such operations as the bottling of the Spanish fleet by Admiral Sampson; for bottling a hostile fleet does not resemble the chance and careless shoving of a cork into a half-used bottle. It is rather like the wiring down of champagne by bonds that cannot be broken, and through which nothing can ooze." Hobson was planning to put in the cork; Admiral Sampson with his blockading fleet must see to the "wiring down."

CABANAS.
(A fortified suburb of Havana.)

The admiral, while approving the young naval constructor's plan, was not altogether confident that the cork would "stay put." If the Spanish admiral determined to escape or to sally out and engage the American fleet, Sampson believed that the way for exit could be made by blowing the wreck to pieces and clearing a path. But if the sinking of the *Merrimac* would only delay things long enough for the American troops to land from the transports without attack, he felt that his purpose would be served. Once get Cervera and his ships even temporarily "bottled up," and the army that was waiting at Tampa could be ferried across with safety and despatch.

By the time Santiago was reached, Mr. Hobson had arranged all the details in his mind, and as the flagship steamed past the *Merrimac*, when coaling one of the warships, he looked closely at what might be his glory or his grave. And when a shot at long range, fired from the *Vizcaya*, fell short of the *New York* and sent the water spurting high, the young naval constructor was brought vividly face to face with the risk of his endeavor, as he sailed thus between cause and effect.

But he had the enterprise close at heart. The admiral had promised him the leadership, and, when once the ground (or rather the water) had been inspected and the course decided upon, two hundred men were set to work stripping the *Merrimac* of everything except the coal and the bulky chains and anchors that would help to sink her when once she was exploded.

No one was to be ordered on this mission, and Mr. Hobson had decided that with six men as assistants he could carry out his plan. Six volunteers were called for; five hundred at once responded. From every ship in the squadron came requests, appeals, and demands to be allowed to go. From captains to coal passers, from middies to marines, came the response: "I'm ready;" until, as Mr. Hobson declares, " It may be said broadly that the bulk of the fleet was anxious to go."

But only six could go — young, athletic, vigorous fellows, used to exposure, cool-headed, and under absolute discipline. These at last were selected from the rush of applicants, and very soon everything was ready for the enterprise. The *Merrimac* was stripped, the coal shifted, the great anchors at bow and stern slung and lashed, the double bottom weighted with seven hundred tons of water, the sea-connections prepared for instant opening, the seven torpedoes attached and connected by electric wires to the button on the bridge, the men all instructed as to their respective duties. Then, after one false start had been made and recalled, at last, at three o'clock on the morning of June 3, the good-bys were said and the great collier, doomed to destruction, steamed away from the fleet. Straight on she sailed, and in the track of the moonlight crept into the long and narrow entrance of Santiago harbor, bound on her enterprise of daring and of possible death.

The volunteer crew, increased at the last moment to seven, all understood their duties. Daniel Montague, chief master-at-arms on the *New York*, was to cut the lashing and let go the stern anchor;

J. E. Murphy, coxswain of the *Iowa*, was to cut the lashing and let go the bow anchor, and then, passing over to the port side, connect Torpedo No. 1 to fire; George Charette, gunner's mate on the *New York*, was to attend to Torpedoes 2 and 3; Oscar Deignan, coxswain of the *Merrimac*, was to attend to Torpedo 4; John P. Phillips, machinist on the *Merrimac*, Torpedo 6; Francis Kelly, water-tender on the *Merrimac*, Torpedo 7; and Rudolph Clausen, coxswain on the *New York*, the seventh man of the crew, selected on the spur of the moment by Mr. Hobson, was to be steersman until relieved at the wheel by young Deignan, when he was to rush over and connect Torpedo 5. Before attending to their torpedoes Phillips and Kelly, who were in the engine-room, were to stop the engine, open the sea-connections so as to fill the hull with water, and then stand by to fire their torpedoes. If the torpedoes were fired as arranged, the *Merrimac* would go down, bow on, and the wreck would be complete. Uniforms were stripped off, revolver-belts and life-preservers strapped on, and with the gallant Hobson on the bridge, directing everything, the *Merrimac* stole into the shadow of the rugged height crowned by the formidable fortifications of Morro.

Nearer and nearer they crept; the channel was not fifteen hundred feet away; once in that the headway and flood-tide would carry them to the selected spot, in spite of fort and battery.

They were just wondering why they were so long unmolested, when out from the water came a flash of fire. A picket boat had opened on the great black intruder; another and another shot rang out, then with a crash the western battery began to play upon them. But Morro Point, where the deep-water channel ran, was but two ship-lengths off. Then Hobson gave the signal to the men below; the engines were stopped; the water connections were thrown open; the *Merrimac* began to fill and settle.

" Down to your torpedoes! " ordered Hobson; the *Merrimac* entered the channel, while from every battery flashed the flame and shot. Morro rock was only thirty feet away, but the big collier still minded her helm, and with a sheer to starboard Morro rock was passed and the point aimed at was but half a ship-length off.

Then came the order " hard aport! " but alas, the ship did not answer to young Deignan's touch, though he brought the helm hard aport and lashed it fast. Then, just at the edge of success, came

BOTTLING UP THE FLEET AT SANTIAGO

defeat. A shot had carried away the steering-gear, and they had missed their position.

Seven thousand tons of unmanageable wood and iron were adrift, with but two anchors to hold them in place! A signal from the bridge, and Murphy let fall the bow anchor; another instant, and with a smothered roar his torpedo was exploded and a great rent torn in the forward part.

With that, from every Spanish battery on shore and height came the storm of shot and shell. They thought a Yankee cruiser, crowded with men and bristling with guns, was forcing the harbor. In the midst of all the roar and fire Hobson stood on the bridge with his hands megaphoned about his mouth, shouting again and again the order: —

"Fire all torpedoes!"

There was no response; his signal cord was useless; Torpedoes 2 and 3 did not follow suit. Then up rushed Charette. "They won't fire, sir; the cells are shattered."

Two then were useless; but No. 5 was all right, and Clausen rang it out with good effect. Of the others, the connection had been shot away and the cells shattered. Only two torpedoes had done their duty.

Just then the settling collier drifted off Estrella

Point, the spot where the channel is narrowest and which Hobson and the admiral had selected as the sinking-place. Instead of shattering and sinking the collier at once, the two torpedoes had only partially accomplished the destruction that should have been swift to be effective.

"Let go the stern anchor!" That was to be Montague's work; but the lashings of the stern anchor had been shot away, and only the bow anchor was down; alas! that dragged, and the tide slowly drifted the *Merrimac* off Estrella Point.

Crash! boom! bang! Every battery joined in the chorus of destruction as machine and rapid-fire guns and all the furies of modern artillery broke upon the doomed collier. Spanish regiments lined the eastern and western shores, to repel the intruder, their repeating rifles cracking incessantly. Then came a shock from below. A Spanish mine had exploded and had done the work of the ruined and useless Yankee torpedoes, while, hidden in the shadows, protected by the bulwarks, those eight brave Americans floated through that shattering fire and calmly arranged just how they should drop from the wreck at just the right moment.

"Not a man moved," says Mr. Hobson, "not even when a projectile plunged into the boiler,

HOBSON ON THE BRIDGE OF THE MERRIMAC.

(With his hands megaphoned about his mouth, he shouted, again and again, "Fire all torpedoes!")

BOTTLING UP THE FLEET AT SANTIAGO 127

and a rush of steam came up the deck not far from where we lay." That is the effect of the superb discipline of the American navy!

Sinking slowly, the *Merrimac* drifted from the desired "corking spot" off Estrella Point, out into the widening channel, on between two Spanish torpedo boats coming at her from either side. Then, with a terrible lurch to port, head on, the big collier plunged to its death; the stern rose, keeled, shivered, and sank, and as the water came pouring over the deck, the eight heroes were swept over by the sea, and the next instant were climbing to the floating catamaran or life-raft — for the life-boat had been shot away. Thus they floated out of the whirlpool about the sinking *Merrimac*, unharmed, save for slight bruises from drifting wreckage — a miraculous instance of pluck combined with good fortune.

Clinging to the catamaran, with only their heads above water, they floated about until daylight, singularly unobserved by the Spanish soldiers on shore, or the searchers in the boats that pulled about the wreck. Then, as broad daylight burst above the heights of Santiago, a steam launch bore down upon them, her forecastle crowded with Spanish riflemen.

"Load! ready! aim!" the command sounded clear in the morning air. But the command to fire did not follow. For Hobson called out: —

"Is there an officer in that launch? An American officer wishes to surrender himself and his seamen as prisoners of war."

The curtains parted; a gray-haired officer looked out; the rifles were ordered down, and Admiral Cervera, commander of the Spanish squadron, leaning far out, helped into the launch the bold young naval constructor who had attempted, by sinking the *Merrimac*, to "wire down" the cork in Admiral Sampson's bottle.

One by one the other seamen were drawn aboard.

"You are brave fellows," exclaimed the Spanish admiral, with genuine appreciation of a glorious endeavor, while the launch, steaming back to the Spanish fleet, set Hobson on board the *Reina Mercedes* and delivered over the eight heroes of the *Merrimac* as prisoners of war.

This valiant act of Hobson and his comrades, as President McKinley truthfully asserted, "thrilled not alone the hearts of our countrymen, but the world, by its exceptional heroism." And just as truthfully did the President say, "It is a most gratifying incident of the war that the bravery of this little band of heroes was cordially appreciated by the Spanish admiral, who sent a flag of truce to notify Admiral Sampson of their safety and to compliment them on their daring act."

WHERE THE MERRIMAC LIES.

(Just beyond Estrella Point in Santiago harbor. The smokestack of the sunken collier just shows above the water.)

But the big collier, broken and destroyed in the interests of naval necessity, rested, a sunken wreck, upon the yellow sands of Santiago harbor. She had not gone down in the precise spot desired, but the endeavor had been alike brave and skilful, and showed the Spaniards that, having once bottled them up in Santiago harbor, the American blockaders intended to keep them there, even at the sacrifice of costly iron ships and brave Yankee seamen.

CHAPTER VII

HOW THE MARINES HELD THE BEACH AT GUANTA-
NAMO

WHEN Cadet Powell, of the *New York*, who, with a pluck and courage fully the equal of that of Hobson and his men, had crept along in the wake of the *Merrimac* and waited, in the face of the Spanish fire, to rescue Hobson's crew after the explosion, came on board the flagship, he reported to the anxious admiral that the *Merrimac* had sunk beyond Estrella Point.

"But not a man came back, sir," he said sorrowfully. "I waited until daylight, hoping to pick up one of them swimming our way; but not one showed up, and we had to come out without them, under fire of the batteries."

It was a brave and generous, as it was a hazardous, deed for the young ensign and his volunteer crew. But the admiral had not believed that in the attempt to sink the *Merrimac* the risk of death was so great as others held it to be.

"It is a dangerous thing to do," he said, "and a brave thing. But I think they have a good chance. It isn't so easy to shoot eight men on a big ship on a dark night; and you know," he added, "the Spaniards are very poor shots.".

But when Ensign Powell reported that no one came back, the admiral was deeply exercised over the fate of his eight brave volunteers,— some of whom had actually thanked him for the privilege of thus going into terrible danger. So, when that same afternoon Admiral Cervera's chief of staff came to the *New York*, under a flag of truce, with a letter from the Spanish admiral to the American admiral reporting that the "brave young Americans" were all safe and would be treated as prisoners of war, Admiral Sampson was greatly relieved, and said in his report to the Navy Department: "I cannot myself too earnestly express my appreciation of the conduct of Mr. Hobson and his gallant crew. I venture to say that a more brave and daring deed has not been done since Cushing blew up the *Albemarle*."

But the cork in the bottle, though bravely jammed in by Hobson and his men, had not, as Captain Mahan puts it, been securely "wired down." It was necessary, therefore, to blockade the entrance to Santiago harbor effectually and also to cripple or silence the Spanish batteries that guarded the approach to the harbor.

HOBSON'S INTERPRETER.

(One of the "boys" at the front "interviewing" the man who acted as Hobson's interpreter in prison.)

From the sea-battery above the cave under Morro to the Gorda battery, within range of whose guns the *Merrimac* finally sank, there were ten forts, batteries, and mine stations protecting the entrance to Santiago. These the admiral determined to silence, or, at least, so to injure them as to make it safe for a battleship to lie close inshore. For Admiral Sampson, like Commodore Dewey, had been one of "Farragut's boys," and, under the tuition of that great admiral, he had learned the wisdom of Farragut's highly practical, if warlike, assertion that "the best protection against an enemy's fire is a well-directed fire from our own guns."

This aggressive protection Admiral Sampson was vigilant to secure alike against enemies on sea and enemies on shore. So, while mindful of the Navy Department's warning not to risk ships against fortifications, the admiral, who had already tried the temper and tested the marksmanship of the Spanish gunners, proceeded to enforce protection by Farragut's method.

On the morning of the sixth of June, in the midst of drifting and curtain-like rain-squalls, the fleet, dividing into two sections, one under command of Admiral Sampson, the other led by Commodore Schley, headed inshore and attacked, with a relentless fire, the eastern and western sides of the harbor respectively.

They steamed to within less than a mile from

shore; they raked the forts and batteries on either side, while shells from the flagship were even dropped upon the Gorda battery at the head of the channel and swept the Spanish torpedo boat, the *Reina Mercedes*, with a rain of death. The drifting mist and the dense cannon smoke mingled in an almost impenetrable cloud, but for nearly three hours the terrible bombardment continued until at last the forts were silenced, and the fleet, having secured what might be termed "Farragut protection" by Farragut rules, obeyed the signal "cease firing" and dropped back to its station on blockade.

How effectual was the "protection" thus secured may be seen from the assertion of Captain Chadwick of the *New York* that during the month of blockade not a shot was fired by the enemy at any one of the blockading fleet.

That this bombardment of the Santiago batteries should have been accomplished without injury to the American squadron is almost marvellous, especially if we accept the sea-statement that one gun mounted on shore is worth several on board ship. For, as you know, Sampson's attacking fleet came within less than a mile of shore, and, upon one of the principal batteries — known as the Socapa battery — Hobson himself counted "emplacements" for eleven mortars, rapid-fire, and revolving cannon, up-to-date in construction and powerful in their capacity for destruction. And yet, in that bombardment, not one of our ships was hurt. It was the difference between training and inefficiency in the men behind the guns on fleet and shore.

Having by this energetic method secured that freedom from molestation while on blockade, Admiral Sampson next proceeded to get possession of a desirable harbor on shore, where he could establish a base of supplies for his fleet, and also maintain a coaling-station, which would render it unnecessary to make the long voyage to Key West whenever it was necessary to "coal up" his warships.

Such a safe and desirable harbor he had discovered at Guantanamo Bay, — an island-protected harbor, thirty-eight miles to the east of Santiago, with good and safe anchorage well inshore, a shelter from hurricane, storm, and attack, and just the place for a supply, repair, and coaling station.

There were in this bay an inner and an outer harbor. The admiral first despatched two well-tried commanders — McCalla in the cruiser *Mar-*

blehead and Brownson in the auxiliary cruiser *Yankee*—to force and occupy the outer bay at Guantanamo. This they proceeded to do with their customary thoroughness, raking the Spanish battery planted at the entrance, driving the supporting gunboat scudding to cover, and scattering the artillerists and soldiers along shore.

While this was on foot, there were on the way from Key West six hundred United States marines, —those "horse-sailors" of the navy, of whom little is ever said, but upon whom depends much of the guardianship, discipline, and efficiency of the navy, in times of peace as well as in days of war.

It was at noonday of the tenth of June that Colonel Huntington and his six hundred marines (including one artillery company) sailed into Guantanamo Bay upon the transport *Panther*, to make the first armed landing and establish the first real American camp on Cuban soil. To support their attempt the *Oregon* and the *Yankee*, the *Yosemite* and the *Scorpion*, warships large and small, escorted the *Panther*, as also the despatch boat *Dolphin* and the store-ship *Supply*.

Thanks to the visit of the *Marblehead*, no resistance was offered to the landing of the marines as they pulled ashore in small boats and landed on

THE MARINES AT GUANTANAMO 137

the beach just inside the eastern point of the harbor. They landed with cheers and music, and Sergeant Silver of Company C, first battalion of Marines, forthwith raced up the hill that rose from the beach and over the ruins of a battered Spanish blockhouse ran up the stars and stripes, — the first raising of the starry banner by an armed force on the debatable ground of Cuba. On this hill the marines at once proceeded to establish their camp, which, in honor of the bold captain of the *Marblehead* who had prepared the way, they christened Camp McCalla.

But the Spaniards had been gathering in force in the brush beyond the hill, determined to resist this forcible occupation by "Yankee pigs." With customary Spanish procrastination, however, they delayed the attack until the marines were comfortably settled and quite "at home" in Camp McCalla. They might have annoyed and retarded the landing of men and supplies, but they did not — perhaps from a pardonable fear of the guns of the Yankee warships which floated just in range of the camp.

At half-past five, however, on the afternoon of June 11, while some of the marines were having a swim, and the rest were taking things easy in camp, two thousand and more of the soldiers of Spain, screened by the thick brush beyond the camp, began a fierce "gunning" of the marines. Up the hill dashed the bathers, scarcely waiting to get into their clothes, and in an instant the well-drilled marines were "peppering" their hidden foe, while scouting parties were sent into the brush to scatter the ambushed enemy.

The enemy was driven from ambush, though two of the marines fell dead in the brush; but at night the Spaniards returned to the attack, pouring in a withering rifle fire at the camp on the hill.

The fight continued all night, and as the brush furnished a perfect ambush for the attacking force, Colonel Huntington decided that discretion was really the better part of valor, and next day proceeded to change camp from the exposed hill-crest to the protected beach. The removal was accomplished during a hot day, under a hot fire, for the Spaniards, counting the removal as a retreat, poured a persistent fire upon the toiling marines. Hiding in the brush, or wrapped in green branches and palm-leaves, so that they were completely disguised, the Spanish assailants, firing their smokeless powder, were no sort of targets for the American marines. They fought bravely,

THE MARINES AT GUANTANAMO.

("The well-drilled marines were peppering their hidden foe.")

however, by raid and dash, while the warships, now increased by the *Texas*, helped the marines, shelling the brush, — though the brush was really all they could shell, for not a Spanish head could be seen.

Men dropped under the hot but unskilful fire of the Spanish riflemen, and, as delays are dangerous in the unhealthy Cuban summer, the burial of the dead was forced to take place in the face of Spanish assault. This even increased to a furious and dangerous fire, turned upon the groups gathered about the graves of the dead marines. From every convenient vantage point the riflemen poured in their steady fire, which might have been tragic and terrible in its results, had only the Spanish soldiers known how to shoot.

This invasion of all the rights and decencies of civilized warfare, however, simply infuriated the marines who were paying the last honors to their dead comrades, and they obeyed the order to repel their assailants with a will and a vigor that speedily drove the Spaniards out of ambush and out of range.

They were persistent, however, those Spanish ambuscaders. No sooner were they driven away, than, after a little rest, they returned again to their cover; they came by day and they came by night, giving the marines little rest and keeping the ships' gunners busy, through a week of ceaseless brush fighting.

At last, Colonel Huntington saw that he must drive off the Spaniards, or his camp on the beach would be untenable. Learning from Cuban scouts where the Spanish fighting base was located, he ordered out all his marines, forced a passage through the thick brush, pushing the still unseen Spaniards back from ridge to ridge, back from the shore to their supply station. Here the enemy, making no concerted stand, broke and ran seaward again; but the despatch boat *Dolphin* saw them coming over the hills, and drove them back, until, caught between marines, *Dolphin*, and Cuban allies, certain of the encompassed Spaniards surrendered, while the rest, under cover of the brush, escaped altogether.

Thereupon the warships in the bay reduced the forts in the upper bay and "cleaned out" the town of Caimanera at the head of the harbor. Possession was complete, and from that time to the end of the war the United States government, thanks to the pluck and persistence of the unheralded and modest marines, held the bay and harbor of Guantanamo as a base and supply station, of inestimable help and value in the tedious but efficient work of the blockading squadron at Santiago.

How tedious and wearing this was, the records of that month of ceaseless watching bear witness.

Day and night that vigilance never relaxed. By day, six miles off the Morro, floated the semicircle of stern and frowning warships, saying to the Spanish admiral, "Stay in!" By night, two miles nearer shore, while the picket ends of the deadly semicircle were but a mile from the Spanish batteries, the big and little ships swung to the tide or the wind, saying to the Spanish admiral, "Come out if you dare!"

Would he dare? Santiago had been but a port of refuge to him on his way to the relief of Havana. But that port of refuge had proved a prison. Would he dare "break jail"?

It would be a risky thing to do while Sampson and his watch-dogs waited outside. For to all his squadron the American admiral issued this significant order: "If the enemy tries to escape, the ships must close and engage as soon as possible, and endeavor to sink his vessels or force them to run ashore in the channel. . . . The escape of the

Spanish vessels at this juncture would be a serious blow to our prestige and to a speedy end of the war."

All day the lookouts in the tops watched the opening to the flask-like harbor; all night, from one or more great battleships, the search-lights made the entrance as bright as day, until the Spanish soldiers on Morro were well-nigh blinded and crazed with the steady glare, and even the men on the entrapped Spanish fleet and in the forts far up the harbor blinked and chafed under this never ending surveillance.

The unbroken strain of watching told, too, on the blue-jackets and middies of the blockading fleet. The men in the picket boats — mostly steam launches or torpedo boats — never knew how soon the gunners in the Spanish batteries or the riflemen on the beach might open fire on them, while the shifting and impenetrable night shadows outside the circle of the electric lights were so full of possible danger that launches and even warships were, at times, "rattled" enough to bombard the caves under Morro, mistaking them for a slowly moving, densely shadowed Spanish hull, or to plunge a nervous and scattering fire into the surf, breaking white against the cliffs, confident that it was the "bone in the teeth" of some escaping warship or torpedo boat of Spain.

Watching is weary business. Again and again the jackies in the squadron grumbled at delay and demanded action; just as "in the States" the people fretted at delay. But Admiral Sampson knew

MORRO CASTLE, SANTIAGO.

(Here Hobson was first imprisoned. Near this cave under the castle Powell was to wait for Hobson, and this cave was bombarded by the fleet, mistaking the shadow for a Spanish hull.)

his duty; the Navy Department recognized its responsibilities; the War Board and the President would not depart from their plans. The capture and occupation of Porto Rico, a dash at the Canaries, even the bombardment of Spain's own coast, all of which an unskilled press and an unreasoning public frequently demanded, were not the things to be done. The object of the war, the reason for all this blockading by the navy and massing of troops by the army, was but the one demand to Spain: "Get out of Cuba! and get out now!"

"As the avowed purpose and cause of our action," says Captain Mahan, greatest of living sea-strategists, "were not primarily redress for grievances of the United States against Spain, but to enforce the departure of the latter from Cuba, it followed logically that the island became the objective of our military movements, as its deliverance from oppression was the object of the war."

It was to keep the Spaniards blockaded in Cuba that the naval vessels of the United States encircled that "ever faithful isle"; it was to prevent assistance or reënforcements from Spain coming to the aid of the beleaguered Spaniards, that the blockade was so rigorously maintained, and it was necessary, especially at Santiago, that the "corralled" Spanish cruiser should be kept "bottled up" by a blockade exceptionally and watchfully rigorous; it was to permit assistance to go to the insurgent Cubans and the starving reconcentrados that the warships closed fast about the island, protecting the frequent landing alike of arms and supplies for the Cubans; but, especially, the naval operations were centred in Cuban waters in order that, under the convoy of the warships and under the protection of their guns, the soldiers of the United States, now massing in camps of instruction or in camps of concentration, might be carried in the big black transports across the blue water that lay between Florida and Cuba, where, once safely landed, they should proceed, as vigorously as Yankee boys in blue and brown know how, "to enforce the President's demand that Spain at once relinquish its authority and government in the island of Cuba, and withdraw its land and naval forces from Cuba and Cuban waters. . . ." In other words, as said above, Spain was to get out at once, or be forced out.

One Spanish fleet was entrapped at Santiago; but another Spanish fleet was known to be ready for action at Cadiz; and though it was said to be ordered to Manila to "smash Dewey," there was still a possibility that it might make a sudden dash across the Atlantic and either threaten the coast towns, destroy the transports, or relieve Cervera. Besides these warships there were known to be in Havana harbor and at San Juan in Porto Rico certain small Spanish cruisers, gunboats, and torpedo boats, which, while of no avail against the American warships, might crawl out of their retreats in the darkness, and, sneaking along by devious ways and secret means, intercept the transports on their way across to Cuba, and with a sudden dash or a stab in the dark send many brave boys in unprotected ships down to " Davy Jones's locker."

So, while the first military expedition was preparing to embark for Cuba on a war of invasion, — a new duty for American soldiers, — watchfulness on the seas and uncertainty as to the real whereabouts of certain wandering Spanish ships of war became suddenly magnified into fear for the safety of the transports, as rumors of a squadron of phantom cruisers, — " the spook fleet," as it came to be called, — delayed the embarkation and complicated matters.

We laugh at it, now that the war is a thing of the past, and smile at the fear that held back an army because of a phantom fleet that never had any existence, save in the imagination of certain over-cautious skippers who made a destroying enemy out of equally cautious friends who did not return sea-signals. But had their over-caution been presumption instead, and their phantom fleet been a real one, not all the excuses that might have been framed would have satisfied the country for the loss of even one transport and her precious freight. Even if Falstaff the boaster did say it, "the better part of valor is indeed discretion," — a truth which men and nations, often through hard experience, have to learn, as well as boys, boards of strategy, and captains of warships.

CHAPTER VIII

WHY THE BOYS CHEERED AT DAIQUIRI

Copyright, 1898, by B. J. Falk, N.Y.
GENERAL SHAFTER.

"FOR a short, rough-and-ready, dashing campaign, such as this bids fair to be, the best man to lead is General Shafter."

Thus the commanding general is said to have reported to the War Department. Whether or not he did so recommend in precisely the words ascribed to him, it is certain that the War Department, upon his advice, did appoint Major-General William R. Shafter, commanding the Fifth Corps, U.S.A., as leader of the expedition ordered to the invasion of Cuba — twenty thousand men in all, regulars and volunteers, gathered in camp at or near Tampa, on the west coast of Florida.

General Shafter was a big, bluff, sturdy soldier of the bull-dog type, with a head that suggested persistence, and a will that made him the typical drive-ahead, rough-and-ready fighter. He was a veteran of the Civil War, in which he made a record for tenacity, bravery, and force, and it was believed that his leadership would insure a brief, vigorous, and successful campaign.

But would that campaign ever begin? So queried the volunteers and regulars in camp at Tampa; the officers of all ranks and degrees, alike in the company streets of the camp and on the broad piazzas of the gorgeous hotel at Tampa; the impatient recruits and veterans in all the other camps, state and national; and the waiting, anxious people at home.

No one really could answer truthfully, for the beginnings of a war are always uncertain. There are so many necessary, but halting, details, — enlistment, discipline, equipment, supply, health and comfort, — so many questions as to selection, route, transportation, landing, and forage, so many problems of plan, destination, and security, that decision comes slowly and action, at first, always drags.

Here was an army of two hundred thousand men to be handled, and the actual experience in war was limited to comparatively few of those who were preparing to invade, in summer time, a land where the summer is apt to be a burdensome, dangerous, and even deadly season to those who come from the north.

The other camps all were eager for the fray — eager, yet unprepared for it; but in the camp of concentration at Tampa, from which the first move was to be made, matters were even more uncertain and unprepared, because with the unpreparedness was mingled the snarl of conflicting departments — commissary, medical, engineer's, and the rest. But, even while waiting for orders, things were put into some sort of shape, and when at last the command " Forward! March!" was issued, the army at Tampa was too glad to be up and doing, to criticise, at that time, the lack of sufficient accommodation or the shortcomings in the way of transportation, comfort, and food.

For days the query had been, " Where are we going, anyhow?" coupled with the impatient demand, "and when?" Some said it was to be to Porto Rico, some to Santiago, some even expected it to be "On to Havana!" But those who dreaded the evils of a Cuban summer, while

WHY THE BOYS CHEERED AT DAIQUIRI 153

anxious to act, believed that the government would be satisfied with a naval blockade and wait until the healthy season — the fall — for an actual invasion and a military campaign.

There came, however, on the seventh of June, a despatch from Admiral Sampson to the Secretary of the Navy.

"Bombarded the forts at Santiago, to-day," he reported. "Have silenced works quickly without injury of any kind. . . . If ten thousand men were here, city and fleet would be ours within forty-eight hours. Every consideration demands immediate army movement. If delayed, city will be defended more strongly by guns taken from fleet."

That despatch brought immediate action. There was a hurried consultation at Washington. Orders were rushed to Tampa. The army broke camp at once, and by daylight of Wednesday, June 8, it was at Port Tampa, nine miles away, ready to go aboard the transports.

But no sooner were all the troops embarked, than there sprang up fears of the "phantom fleet" which, as I have told you, was reported as roaming about the coast on the watch for just such game as defenceless transports loaded with American soldiers. These fears kept the expedition in port until they were proved groundless, but at last, on the morning of Tuesday, the fourteenth of June, the order came to get under way, and, casting off its moorings at Port Tampa, the Fifth Army Corps, with its naval escort, sailed in a long, uneven, triple column across a motionless, indigo sea, headed at last for the invasion of Cuba —

AT THE DOCK AT TAMPA.
(Transport *Concho* loading for Cuba.)

"the largest number of United States troops that ever went down to the sea in ships to invade a foreign country."

Fifty-four ships, counting the escort of war-vessels, comprised this modern armada. Upon the transports were embarked an army of very nearly seventeen thousand men, with Major-General Will-

WHY THE BOYS CHEERED AT DAIQUIRI

iam R. Shafter in command. It consisted of the Fifth Army Corps, a battalion of engineers, a detachment of the signal corps, twelve squadrons of unmounted cavalry, four batteries of light artillery, two batteries of heavy artillery, and an independent brigade of regular infantry.

Admiral Sampson's despatch was as justifiable as it was urgent. The plan of the War Board at Washington was to have the army and navy work together for the occupation and reduction of Cuba. The admiral had brought things just to the "coöperating point," and if that miserable "spook fleet" of Spain, which never really existed, had not gone cruising around like a nineteenth century "Flying Dutchman," and driven the transports back to shelter, the army and navy would have joined hands at once; forty-eight hours' work would have captured Santiago, and the delay the admiral feared would not have led to the complication that did result. But, as General Grant said, "the only eyes a general can trust are his own," and if those eyes cannot pierce an uncertainty, it is unwise to risk too much. So the embarkation was delayed for a week, and the old rule was again proven true, "Delays are dangerous."

The War Board had endeavored to prepare the way, and the Secretary of the Navy had informed the admiral that the seventeen thousand men embarking at Port Tampa were destined for Santiago. He requested the admiral to select suitable landing-places near Santiago and especially to secure the pier at Daiquiri.

Now this Daiquiri (or Baiquiri, as it is sometimes spelled) is the name of a little river in southeastern Cuba, at the mouth of which, eighteen miles to the east of Santiago, stood the machine shops and the ore-dock of a big iron company. This was the pier at Daiquiri. A few palm-thatched huts, in which the company's workmen lived, clustered about the pier, and behind the little settlement rose the foothills of the Uraguacita Mountains, backed by the mountains themselves.

This place, it was claimed, was the most reasonable way by which to march an army to the investment of Santiago, making the capture of the city itself rather than of the forts at the mouth of the harbor the work laid out for the army. For this was the plan of coöperation: the army was to attack the city in the rear, while the navy bombarded the forts at the front, and thus, between

WHY THE BOYS CHEERED AT DAIQUIRI 157

them, crushing all opposition and forcing a speedy surrender.

East by south, until it came abreast the northern coast of Cuba off the province of Puerto Principe, the Yankee Armada sailed; then, skirting the Cuban coast, past Baracoa, it ran through the

THE HEIGHTS OF JIBARA.

(North shore of Santiago province, Cuba. At this point Columbus landed on the shore of Cuba. From an etching by Blaney.)

Windward Passage, rounded Cape Maisi, skirted the southern shore, and at last, at noon, on Monday the twentieth of June, the transports lay in the offing before the ore-pier of Daiquiri.

Despite all the preparations made there were many things lacking in that army of invasion —

cavalrymen without horses, artillerists without guns, doctors without hospital stores, and cooks without food. But it was to be a quick, "rough-and-ready" campaign, and if there were no room for the cavalrymen's horses, no time to embark the guns of the artillery, no chance to get the doctors' medicines, and no opportunity to pick and choose the food, no one should complain. It was more like a big picnic than anything else, and what mattered a little rough-and-tumble experience when it would all be over so soon?

How soon it would be over depended very largely upon how soon General Shafter got at work, and when he and Admiral Sampson met at last on the twentieth of June some twenty miles or so east of Santiago, and after they had gone ashore at Aserraderos, eighteen miles west of Santiago, and had there conferred with the Cuban General Garcia, it was decided to land the invading army at once at the ore-pier at Daiquiri.

To make this landing in safety and to guard against Spanish attempts to repel the invasion, many things had to be provided for. The Cuban allies of the Yankee invaders were relied upon to clear the way and push back the Spaniards from the vicinity of the ore-dock; the beaches, the

WHY THE BOYS CHEERED AT DAIQUIRI 159

BARACOA, NEAR CAPE MAISI.
(The most easterly town of Cuba, in the province of Santiago.)

beach-houses, and the "covers" for three miles to either side and to the rear of the Daiquiri landing, were shelled by the warships to clear them of all intrenched or ambushed Spaniards; and a "false landing" was to be attempted by certain of the transports and their escorts at the bay of Cabanas, two miles or so to the westward of Santiago, in order to draw off and divide the Spanish resistance. Then, when these preliminaries had been attended to, the small boats of the fleet — whale-boats, steam cutters, and all pulling boats from the warships and transports — were to be filled with soldiers and speedily rowed ashore by the blue-jackets, or, rather, the white-jackets, of the fleet.

This may all seem simple enough as you read it, but it was no easy task. Through the clear, cool morning air of that twenty-second of June, 1898, a day to be forever notable in American history, the boom of the guns of the warships lying off the Cuban coast about Santiago thundered out their part of the programme, clearing the shore of would-be Spanish obstacles to possession. Then the fussy little steam launches sped from ship to ship with their string of rocking rowboats, into which the soldiers tumbled, dropped, or sprawled, devoid of the necessary "sea-legs" which the landsman needs to acquire if he is to cut anything but a ridiculous figure on shipboard, and, especially, in the act of boarding a tossing rowboat from the deck of a rocking, unsteady transport. Very few of the soldiers ferried across to Cuba had acquired these necessary "sea-legs"; very many of them had never had sea-experience; some had never even seen the ocean before, and were as innocent of its moods and terms as was that cowboy trooper of the First

WHY THE BOYS CHEERED AT DAIQUIRI

U.S. Volunteer Cavalry (popularly known as Roosevelt's "Rough Riders") who, when a strong sea-breeze blew his hat overboard, on the voyage to Cuba, announced to his comrade or "bunkie," "Say, Jim! mah hat fell into the crick!"

The first boats are filled now, and the race for the shore begins. It is not an easy shore for a landing. Upon the sandy stretch of beach the surf tumbles, breaks, and rolls in a fashion not altogether suited to the evolutions of a big keel rowboat; the ore-pier, built for dumping coal into vessels and not for landing passengers from small boats, is too high for use; another small dock beneath it, rickety and unprotected, is also too high for easy landing from small boats; the smoke from the bombardment, which has split and shattered everything on shore from the blazing stack on the beach to the dismantled blockhouse on the heights, wreathes the pitching launches and the crowded rowboats; nose to nose the white whale-boats head for the beach; then a chugging steam launch darts ahead and makes for the lower dock, and as a heavy sea tosses it to the level of the wharf a zealous half dozen troopers who have "got good and ready" take a flying leap, and with a glad hurrah strike the stringers, when with a waving of muskets over their heads they shout each to each and each to all, "First man on shore!"

The whale-boats pull ahead, a long roll of surf carries them well up the coral-strewn beach, and, out of the boats, knee-deep in the tumbling foam, other troopers leap and spring, and with a louder cheer announce "First man on land!"

The cheers from dock and beach are echoed and reëchoed from rowboat, launch, and transport; other boats pull into the surf or toss their men upon the rickety dock; squad after squad is landed, while tossing hats and ringing cheers tell that the long suspense is broken, and that the army of liberation is at last really on Cuban soil, ready for the duty of delivering it from its four hundred years of slavery and oppression.

But in the midst of all the shouts and scramble of an invading army, up the trail that threads the hill behind Daiquiri, four men are racing with a purpose that has been theirs since first, from their dancing keel boats, they spied the empty flagpole that tops the Spanish blockhouse on the crest of the ridge. Now they come into view beside it, dwarfed by distance, and all their comrades on ship and shore divine their purpose. A moment only they pause; then, pulling away at the clicking halyards, a bit of bunting climbs the empty pole; another instant and the stars and stripes flutter in the breeze, hauled aloft by vigorous and determined hands; then the soft but steady sea-breeze borne in from Cuban waters catches the folds of red and white and blue, and straight out from the top of its Spanish staff streams the American flag, dear to millions of hearts, the symbol of liberty, humanity, occupation and liberation, the notice to Spain that, as the President of the United States had declared, "In the name of humanity, the intolerable conditions in Cuba must cease!"

And as the glorious stars and stripes fluttered out from the Spanish flagstaff, all the pent-up enthusiasm of regular and volunteer, of "doughboy" and "jackie," of landsman and seaman, of commander and commanded, of fighting man and non-combatant, of Yankee trooper and Cuban ally, of the liberator and the liberated, burst into one mighty chorus of cheers, which, mingling with the shrill clangor of steam whistles on launch and transport and warship, filled all the soft Cuban air with one long, vociferous, joyful, deafening salute to "Old Glory," streaming out above the captured blockhouse on the green heights above the sea-beach of Daiquiri.

Unopposed they had scored their first success. "The country," says Colonel Roosevelt, "would have offered very great difficulties to an attacking force had there been resistance. It was little but a mass of rugged and precipitous hills, covered for the most part by dense jungle. Five hundred resolute men could have prevented the disembarkation at very little cost to themselves." But Spanish resolution was lacking; the occupation of Cuba had been accomplished; the army of liberation had gained an unopposed footing on Cuban soil, and Spain had made one more of its many mistakes through its fear of Yankee gunners and its distrust of its own defenders.

CHAPTER IX

HOW THEY CLEARED THE JUNGLE AT GUASIMAS

Copyright, 1898, by B. J. Falk, N.Y.
COLONEL ROOSEVELT.

THE landing was accomplished; now for the "Forward, march!" The "Rough Riders" of Wood's First Cavalry had hoisted the flag on the blockhouse at Daiquiri; now the army must press on until it had raised the stars and stripes above the conquered defences of Santiago.

The work before our soldier boys of '98 was no child's play. Santiago lay behind its fortifications eighteen miles away. It was protected on the water side by a Spanish fleet and a chain of Spanish forts; on the land side it was defended by embankments and blockhouses, big forts and trenches, and miles of entangling wire fences, while, between these and the American army there were streams to be forded, jungles to be cleared, and embattled heights to be won, as, one above the other, the terraced foothills of the Uraguacita Mountains reared themselves as a series of natural ramparts between Santiago and the sea.

But there is no such abbreviated obstacle as "can't" in the "bright lexicon" of America, from liberating a people to governing a world; and with such a "rough-and-ready" commander as General Shafter — "Bull Shafter" they used to call him in the army — what was to be done must be done and done quickly. Little things, like easy landing, comfort in camp, and "luxuries" on the march, were not to be considered by him when there was work to be accomplished, demanding instant action and heroic measures. The jungle must be cleared, the terraces must be won, the road to Santiago must be kept open from the sea, the American army must at once encompass the beleaguered city on the land in order to hasten the final blow from the blockading fleet on the sea. The work admitted of no hesitation and of no delay, and at once General Shafter set out to demonstrate that geometrical axiom, that a straight line is the shortest distance between two points — one point was at Daiquiri, the other was at Santiago.

HOW THEY CLEARED THE JUNGLE 167

I remember, when I was a boy, planning a vacation walk from New York to Boston. There were three of us in the party, and, boy-like, we desired even a vacation walk to be by the most direct route; so we laid a ruler on the map and drew a straight line between New York and Boston. We followed that straight line, but as I look back at it now, I can see that our straight line "wobbled" a good deal *en route*. It was much

SPANISH "FORTINE," OR FORT NO. 1, OUTSIDE OF SANTIAGO.

the same with the straight line laid down by General Shafter: it "wobbled." With hill and vale, *altar* and *mesa*, creek and jungle, and with Spanish soldiers in Spanish blockhouses on every available height, the straight line must necessarily have been rather ragged and wavering; but of this you may rest assured — it was to lead from Daiquiri to Santiago. And it did!

The first work was to clear the jungle of hostile Spaniards, and open up the road to Santiago, as it wound through the narrow defile, choked by neglect, into little more than an overgrown tropical trail. This road climbed by three ascents the ridges toward Santiago. The valleys it crossed were thick with jungle and chaparral, and laced and netted with vines and creepers, out of which sprang, here and there, palms and banian trees or almost impenetrable hedges of the prickly cactus and the murderous "Spanish bayonets."

To drive the Spaniards from roadway and jungle, the first forward movement was made on the twenty-third of June. At Siboney, nine miles to the west of Daiquiri pier, the transports were still unloading men and tools and supplies on the coral-lined beach, and along the road that led to Siboney General Wheeler advanced from Daiquiri with two squadrons of the First Volunteer Cavalry (the "Rough Riders"), one squadron of the First and one of the Third Regulars and three Hotchkiss guns. The general was anxious to push the fighting. He had "felt" the road and Cuban

HOW THEY CLEARED THE JUNGLE

scouts had told him that the Spaniards were intrenched at a place where two roads from Siboney met to form a wider road, which led into the Santiago highway. General Wheeler's plan was to push forward his picket line and, if possible, dislodge the Spaniards at the fork in the road known as Guasimas, so called from the growth of West Indian elms, or *guazuma* trees, which spring from the jungle at that point.

Out of Siboney, a town of thirty or forty mean little houses, the force destined by General Wheeler to clear the jungle of Spaniards marched, at half-past five o'clock in the morning of June 24, — eight troops of the Rough Riders, five hundred strong (on foot, of course, for their horses, you remember, had been left behind at Tampa). They took a narrow trail-like road which climbed the ridge and led toward Guasimas; half a mile to the right, along a parallel trail known as the Sevilla road, General Young with four troops of the First and four troops of the Tenth Cavalry, two hundred and twenty men in all, were also advancing toward Guasimas. Between the two trails lay a valley thick with brush and jungle. The only artillery in the advance was the three Hotchkiss mountain guns, drawn with General

Young's column. With this column also rode General Wheeler, the commander of the advance.

At half-past seven General Young halted his column in an open glade near to the fork in the roads at Guasimas and there "located" the enemy. At once he unlimbered his battery of mountain guns, sent a Cuban scout across to the other trail to notify Colonel Wood, deployed his column so as to assault in flank, and then directed his attack so that both wings should fight forward to meet at the main point of attack — a stone fort or blockhouse on an angle of the ridge.

Over a mass of hidden vines and creepers, through brush and jungle, cutting through concealed barbed-wire fences and scaling rocky rises toward the ridge, the troopers of the First and Tenth made slow headway, fighting a hidden enemy using smokeless powder, and only to be located in the jungle by the sound and direction of his fire; the two wings came together finally in this jungle maze and together advanced upon the enemy in the face of a continuous fire. Whenever a clear space was reached where the troopers could get anything like a sight of the Spaniards, they would fire in return, but the advance never slackened; not a man fell out, not a straggler lagged behind. "They were led most gallantly," says Colonel Roosevelt, "as American regular officers lead their men; and the men followed their leaders with the splendid courage always shown by the American soldier." So, straight on, those seasoned regulars pressed, until at last the Spaniards could not longer withstand the advance. Turning, they fled precipitately down the slopes, while the cavalrymen occupied the abandoned fortifications, and the heights beyond Siboney were won.

Meantime, along the left-hand trail the Rough Riders marched on to the rendezvous — the fork in the road at Guasimas. In front went Captain Capron and his troop as an advance guard, preceded by Cuban scouts; behind came the colonel and his men in brown. All about them, save on the narrow trail they trod, in single file, stretched the jungle, an almost impenetrable tangle of bush and tree and vine; but no sign of Spanish ambush came, until, suddenly, the advance halted and Colonel Wood, reconnoitring, determined to force the fighting, if any enemy lay concealed in that tangled cover. He, too, as had General Young on the other trail, had "located" the enemy; but here was no open glade for a base of operations. He and his troops were "corralled" in the jungle. Like the veteran fighter he was, however, Colonel Wood proposed to clear that jungle. One troop was ordered to beat the bushes on the right of the trail, the others were sent down into the valley

THE JUNGLE PATH AT GUASIMAS.

("All about them, save on the narrow trail they trod, in single file, stretched the jungle.")

toward Young's column or into the dense growth on the left.

Advancing thus, cautiously, in what is called "open skirmish order," the columns felt the way along until finally, from the jungle, came the heavy Spanish fire and the Rough Riders were in action.

Drilled for cavalry, for fighting on horseback, these volunteer cavalrymen, like the regular cavalrymen in General Young's column, were, as General Shafter declares, equally well drilled to fight on foot, and, as his experience in all Spanish countries had been that there were no roads worthy the name, he had deemed it best to have his cavalry fight dismounted.

The sequel proved the wisdom of his decision; horses would have been well-nigh useless on that narrow, tangled trail; while the trained horsemen of the regular cavalry and of the Rough Riders fought valiantly on foot, and, just as Young's column on the right-hand road was stopped by no obstacle, dismayed by no jungle, and careless as to the number of their opponents, so the men of Wood's column showed equal determination and fought with equal valor.

Slowly advancing, and firing as they advanced, Wood's men pressed the Spaniards steadily back, capturing their blockhouse, forcing their line, and occupying their strong position in the rocks. Then, at last, they saw the Spanish foe, and a heavy fire on both sides followed. Men and officers fell, as they had fallen on the trail, but still the Americans advanced, retaining their excellent order. A withering fire from the ridge above, on which was the rock fort that certain of Young's cavalry were also storming, burst upon the brave Rough Riders; but with a cheer they gained the ridge, and the Spaniards turned in flight. There on the ridge the fighting column of Wood joined the equally victorious troops of Young, and the united columns found themselves victors on the field.

Then their horses at Tampa would have come in well. "Had we possessed any mounted men or even fresh foot troops," said Colonel Wood, "I think we could have captured a large portion of the Spanish force." But the heat and the hard work told on the men, and their task for that day was accomplished. They had cleared the jungle, sent the Spaniards in front flying to their main line, and captured, by persistent and always advancing assault, the height above Siboney. The way for the advance of the army of invasion had been valorously opened, and the fight at Guasimas had been won by the dismounted cavalrymen of Wheeler's brave division.

"There was no ambush, as has been reported," General Shafter says. "The engagement had an inspiring effect on the whole army, showing, as it did, that the Spanish troops could not stand against us, while it proved to our men that they could whip the Spaniards if they could only get at them."

The skirmish at Guasimas had not been won without serious loss. Brave men, white and black, had fallen in the ranks of the fighting cavalrymen, and valuable lives had paid the price of victory. Sixteen killed and fifty-two — one man out of every fourteen engaged — wounded either fatally or severely was the total score. Forty-two of these sixty-eight fell in the ranks of the Rough Riders, who, in the dense jungle of the slopes at Guasimas, were making their first stand and waging their first fight. Those "grim hunters of the mountains, and rough riders of the plains," as Colonel Roosevelt calls them, "had left their lonely hunters' cabins and shifting cow-camps to seek new and more stirring adventures beyond the sea," and with them, also, as volunteer cavalrymen were men of quite another stamp: "recruits," says Colonel Roosevelt, "from Harvard, Yale, Princeton, and many another college; from clubs like the Somerset, of Boston, and Knickerbocker, of New York; and from among the men who belonged neither to club nor to college, but in whose veins the blood stirred with the same impulse which once sent the Vikings over sea."

Of three thousand men, five hundred marched from Siboney to clear the jungle at Guasimas, on the twenty-fourth of June. Of that five hundred, almost one-tenth, forty-two in all, fell

CAMP OF THE ROUGH RIDERS.
(On the battlefield of Guasimas after they had "cleared the jungle.")

wounded or dying on the grassy slope. Chief among these was the gallant Allyn Capron, captain of L troop — "invaluable, from his extraordinary energy, executive capacity, and mastery over men; . . . the ideal of what an American regular army officer should be; in body and mind alike fitted to play his part to perfection — the very archetype of the fighting man," so Colonel Roosevelt assures us. Leading the advance, he first met and repelled the enemy, "and it was in the performance of this duty," runs Colonel Wood's report, "that the captain was mortally wounded. The service he performed prior to his death, and the work of his troops subsequently to it, were of the greatest value in contributing to the success of this engagement."

With him fell Sergeant Hamilton Fish, ex-captain of the Columbia College crew, kin to that Secretary of State who, when the *Virginius* massacre was "adjusted" with Spain, declared that the Cuban problem was certain at some day to lead to blood and war. "'God gives,'" so writes Mr. Davis, "was the motto on the watch I took from his blouse; and God could not have given him a nobler end, — to die in the forefront of the first fight of the war, quickly, painlessly, with a bullet through the heart, with his regiment behind him, and facing the enemies of his country."

Dead and wounded, these thirty-four men marked the Rough Riders' "baptism of blood"; they had fought bravely and were as bravely led. Colonel Wood and his lieutenant-colonel, Theodore Roosevelt, who gave up his post of

Assistant Secretary of the Navy to go "somehow or other to the front and improve the opportunity," as he expressed it, "of driving the Spaniards from the western world," were both praised by their superior officers, Wheeler and Young, and recommended for the promotion that speedily came.

"Both Colonel Wood and Lieutenant-Colonel Roosevelt," ran the report of General Young, "disdained to take advantage of shelter or cover from the enemy's fire while any of their men remained exposed to it; an error of judgment," so the disciplinarian declared, "but, happily," the lover of good fighting hastens to add, "an error on the heroic side."

> "They heard no bugle-peal to thrill,
>   As they crouched in the tangled grass,
> But the sound of bullets whirring shrill
> From hidden hollow and shrouded hill;
> And they fought as only the valiant will,
>   In the glades of Guasimas."

And in General Young's own column — the brave fellows of the First and the "black giants" of the Tenth — was equal valor of leadership and of fighting.

"The behavior of all men of the regular and

HOW THEY CLEARED THE JUNGLE 179

volunteer forces engaged in this action was simply superb," said General Young in his report of the fight, "and I feel highly honored in the command of such troops."

"The brush at Guasimas," as General Shafter calls the first land battle of the war, may have been only a "brush"—not even a skirmish; but it was the test of courage, steadiness, and efficiency in the first hostile encounter of American soldiers on an invaded soil. It may have been premature, as General Shafter intimates when he says that he had intended that Lawton should keep ahead, but that Young's brigade, moving on "in the search for suitable ground," was in the lead of Lawton in marching and attacking the "well-placed Spanish column of observation"; but the report of the dash of the Rough Riders and the steadiness of the "black giants" thrilled the country when the news of the fight was ticked and bulletined all over the land, while, as the optimistic General Wheeler explained in his report, "the engagement at Guasimas inspired our troops and must have had a bad effect upon the spirits of the Spanish soldiers. It also gave our army a beautiful and well-watered country in which we have established our encampments. It has also given us a full view of Santiago and the surrounding country and enabled us to reconnoitre close up to the fortifications of that place."

"The brush at Guasimas" was, therefore, a positive first step in the advance from the sea to Santiago. It had cleared the jungle, won the first of the foothills, opened the way for advanced communication, and, at the cost of brave men's lives and of hurt to brave men's bodies, it had swung armed invasion into open conflict and shown the world that America was ready to back up her word, at any risk and at any cost.

CHAPTER X

HOW THEY BROKE THE LINE AT EL CANEY AND STORMED THE HILL OF SAN JUAN

"THE Yankees were beaten, but they persisted in fighting, and we were obliged to fall back."

So ran the Spanish report of the skirmish at Guasimas on June 24. This experience with Yankee persistence was to continue throughout the campaign in Cuba, in spite of trench and *trocha*, fence and *fortine*, jungle and mudhole, shot and shell, smokeless powder, and malarial fever, as, step by step, ridge after ridge was won, and regulars and volunteers "persisted" in pushing on to the red-tiled roofs and yellow walls of Santiago.

The red roofs and yellow walls of the picturesque old town had already been seen from afar by the scouts and advanced pickets of the American army; for the men who had won the ridge above Guasimas kept it, and for a week their white dog-tents dotted the slope and checkered the vivid green of ridge and *mesa*.

"Keep your front thoroughly picketed and also your right flank and well in advance," said General Shafter to General Wheeler, who was in command at Guasimas; "but do not try any forward movement until further orders."

This forward movement the commanding general wished to be both simultaneous and uniform, and his plan of attack was to flank the Spanish army of defence and get his attacking force between the Spanish troops and Santiago.

"If 1 can get the enemy in my front and the city at my back," said General Shafter, "I can very soon make them surrender or drive them toward the Morro."

And to drive them toward the Morro — the old castle crowning the hill at the narrow entrance to the harbor — would be to drive them straight into the mouths of the waiting guns of the war-fleet.

This manœuvre General Shafter believed would be much better than to attempt an immediate and regular siege of Santiago. He knew the exasperations of a Spanish trail; he recognized the labor of transporting heavy batteries of siege-guns and ponderous ammunition wagons up and over the apologies for roads that crossed the table-lands, swamps, jungles, and ridges that lay between Siboney and Santiago. Shafter was there to force a quick, unrelenting, and persistent assault.

"The sooner it's over, the sooner it's done," was his theory, and hurrying his fresh troops and reenforcements up from the shore he posted his advance line at a sugar plantation called El Pozo,

THE ROAD TO EL CANEY.
(Over which the regulars marched to the battle.)

set up his own headquarters a mile behind the advance, with the most of his army stretching back to the Siboney Road, and then prepared to put his plan into operation.

This plan, as I have explained, was to get between the Spaniards and Santiago. To accomplish this, he proposed to have one brigade hold the road between Santiago and the little town four miles to the northeast of Santiago; this was known as El Caney, and here the Spanish army was strongly posted. This manœuvre would cut off their retreat, while an attack upon the Spanish line in front of Santiago would clear away or capture all the troops outside the eastern defences of the town.

The plan was simple, and would have worked to a charm had there not been other things besides Spanish soldiers in the way.

One of these was a dense forest; beyond that the heights of San Juan, carved into trenches and crowned with blockhouses; two branches or creeks cutting the thick woodland; the village of El Caney, fortified strongly; while every ridge was seamed with trenches and held by Spanish marksmen with their deadly Mauser guns.

That fortified village of El Caney must be taken; those trench-streaked heights of San Juan must be won; and the attacking Americans were but poorly supplied with field artillery, useless in battering down stone ramparts, and too weak for an aggressive assault.

But it would not do to wait for strengthening the artillery line, and at once the right and left

EL CANEY AND SAN JUAN 185

wings were ordered to advance upon the duty assigned them — the right to capture El Caney, the left to assault the lines on San Juan. So, to the right marched Lawton and Chaffee, with Bates's independent brigade of regulars and volunteers, and the small battery of field-guns captained

WHERE THE RIGHT WING MARCHED.
(The road to El Caney. The Spanish fort crowns the hill in the distance.)

by the veteran Capron, father of that gallant captain of the Rough Riders who fell at Guasimas; to the left marched Sumner and Carroll and Wood, with Kent bringing up the rear, while far to the left the supporting column of Duffield, backed by the guns of the fleet, was massed for the attack on the little port of Aguadores.

It was the morning of Friday, the first day of July; regulars and volunteers had trailed off during the night to action, and almost with the day the double battle began.

The duty assigned to Lawton and his men was seemingly easy. When El Caney was cleaned of Spaniards they would march toward Santiago, and, joining Sumner and Kent on the San Juan ridges, the combined forces would proceed to engage and "do up" the Spanish army in front of Santiago.

It seemed easy enough; but things, you know, "are not always what they seem." The American advance had met and defeated the Spaniards at Guasimas; but there the enemy was fighting from ambush, screened by the jungle. Now, the fighting was to be more in the open, and the Spanish defenders were to display a persistent heroism they were not supposed to possess.

Behind the fortifications and within the rifle-pits of El Caney, one thousand Spaniards, under the command of General Vara del Rey, awaited the American advance. Over the stone fort on the hill above El Caney waved the flag of Spain, and, soon after six o'clock on that July morning, the first shot of the battle, flung by "Capron's

Pet," was sent like a challenge at that Spanish flag. Slowly the advance of Lawton's column, the men of Chaffee's brigade, crept over the ridges

"CAPRON'S PET."

(Gun served by Captain Capron of the artillery in his field battery before Santiago.)

toward El Caney, and by eight o'clock they had reached the little thatched town on the hill, in which even the towered church was embattled, while before it and all about it, wherever a trench had been cut, rose a Spanish soldier with his death-dealing Mauser, to pick off the American advance.

Little by little, Lawton's three brigades, led by Chaffee, Miles, and Ludlow, closed in upon the little hill town. But the four light guns of Capron's battery, though persistent and plucky, could scarcely hope to batter down the stone walls of the old stone fort above the town, and until that was taken El Caney would hold out; for General del Rey and his thousand men valiantly stuck to their posts, and died there, as brave men can.

Their Mauser rifles, worked with smokeless powder, were a formidable means of resistance to the American regulars and their Krag-Jorgensen guns. Every step of the advance was dearly paid for, and officers and men dropped under the withering fire from fort, and trenches, and barricaded town.

For four hours the slow advance and fighting at long range went on; then Lawton determined to rush the line, moving Capron's battery closer in, and pushing forward his troopers and infantry by a charge on hill and trenches.

Just at that moment an aide from headquarters came galloping up; another and another followed in quick succession. They bore the commanding general's orders to Lawton, that, as the centre was in danger at San Juan, and the affair at Aguadores had not turned out well, he was to give up the plan of the assault on El Caney, and hasten to the support of the imperilled centre below the heights of San Juan.

"Turn back now?" cried brave Lawton, "now, when to turn would be defeat? See here, Major!" and "about-wheeling" Major Noble, of Shafter's own staff, who had dashed up with the latest orders, the general galloped him along the firing line.

What Major Noble saw led him to modify his orders.

"You're right, General. It's the critical moment; it would be suicide to turn back. Go in and win, and then make your union with Wheeler's division."

Even as he spoke, the order was given. The men had waited in leash too long, exposed to the killing fire of the Mausers, to willingly turn their backs on the final tussle. With a shout the advance began. Ludlow on the left, and Chaffee on the right, dashed to the charge. Ludlow's men carried the Santiago road; a battalion of the Twenty-second Infantry dashed up a hill beyond the road, and covered and prevented the only means of retreat from El Caney to Santiago; while on the right, Chaffee, with a superb dash, sent the Seventh Infantry (half of them recruits, in their first battle) swarming up the hill; like goats the black veterans of the Twenty-fourth closed in on the gallantly defended fort, and as the Spanish flag fell with a well-directed shot, ditch and trench, outwork and fort, were carried by that resistless rush, and El Caney was won.

But at what a cost that "easy duty" was accomplished! Dead and wounded Americans lay scattered before the town and along the slope; dead and wounded Spaniards filled the trenches and the fort. Del Rey, stubborn and brave defender to the last, lay dead amid his officers and

AFTER THE BATTLE.
(The blockhouse or fort at El Caney as it looked after the line was rushed.)

men; while the remnant, laying down the guns with which they had so valiantly stood by their trenches, gave themselves up as prisoners and marched, as they supposed, to certain death.

"Why should we drink?" asked the Spanish corporal, who, with his handful of men, gave up, the last defenders of an outlying blockhouse, as their American captors offered them canteens of water. "Why should we drink when we are about to die?"

"I think you are not to die," replied Major Noble, who, despatched to recall Lawton, had remained to see the final charge; "we are civilized men, and you are brave ones."

Meanwhile the imperilled centre, for whose relief Noble had galloped to Lawton, had wrested victory from disaster. There six regiments of the cavalry division, dismounted troopers all, advanced in extended skirmish line toward the heights of San Juan; after them came the infantry division, while Grimes's battery of field-guns opened fire upon the blockhouse which, like a pagoda, towered above the crest of San Juan hill.

Through underbrush and trees, where the narrowing trail marked the uncertain way, fording the San Juan River and the smaller creek beyond, the cavalry advanced, pushed forward, and there halted to await their comrades, and the union with Lawton's men, who were first to "clear out" El Caney.

But the "clearing out," as you know, was not done in a hurry; for a full hour the centre waited, exposed to a galling fire from blockhouse, trench, and Spanish sharpshooter. To go back was impossible, for the trail was choked with the advanc-

THE SAN JUAN RIVER.
(Which the boys forded on their way to San Juan hill.)

ing rear; to go back was not American when duty lay in front.

Lieutenant Miley, General Shafter's aide, studied the situation.

"The troops should press on in front," he said. "The men along the road are being hit by bullets. The heights must be taken at all hazards. A retreat now would mean a disastrous defeat."

But defeat was the last thing the regulars and Rough Riders could think of or permit. The only way to conquer was to advance. The only escape was, as Mr. Davis says, "by taking the enemy by the throat, driving him out, and beating him down."

"The heights must be taken at all hazards," Lieutenant Miley declared; General Sumner pointed at the blockhouse on the hill of San Juan, which, gorgeously backed by the red foliage of the big tropical tonic shrub which they call the flamboyant tree, stood out a fair and flaming mark.

There was but a moment of indecision. Then, out of the jungle and into the open plain, dashed brave, white-haired General Hawkins and the First Brigade, the Sixth and Sixteenth Infantry, and in the face of a galling fire swept up the hill; there is another rush, and up the hill, mingling with the infantry of Hawkins's Brigade, dash the unmounted troopers of the Tenth Cavalry and the now famous Rough Riders.

Not in serried columns, nor with lowered bayonets, in the fashion of the old-time story-book charges, but singly, and in bunches, low-stooping, fast-creeping, like the Indian fighters that most of them have been, infantryman and trooper, cowboy and football rusher, climb up that deadly slope.

With voice and bugle-call that noble-looking veteran Hawkins led on his men; galloping far ahead, his blue polka-dot handkerchief streaming from his big sombrero like Navarre's oriflamme at Ivry, that embodiment of vigorous young America, Theodore Roosevelt, urged his Rough Riders to their work; hot and fierce in the rain of Mauser bullets from blockhouse and rifle-pits, but up, up, and on, heedless of the fire in front, heedless of the heroes dropping all about them, black and white, regular and Rough Rider, the American soldier charged up the hill; the Spanish soldier reeled backward from trench and blockhouse, and the first height is won.

Then down, under the hill, across the gully and up the other slope, the laboring troopers dash; straight on against the heavily intrenched heights of San Juan, swinging now to the right, where, down from the "bloody angle" rains the leaden hail; against it, over it, into it, while the brave but overmastered Spaniards, unused to such determined onsets, drop everything and flee wildly from the crest; then, at last, above that crest the stars and stripes stream out in token of victory, and the height of San Juan, the key to Santiago's safety, is won.

"I ordered a charge, and the men rushed the

THE CHARGE UP SAN JUAN HILL.

("Not in serried columns, but singly, and in bunches, low-stooping, fast-creeping, they climb the deadly slope.")

blockhouses and rifle-pits on the hill in fine shape," said Roosevelt's simple report. "We then opened fire on the intrenchments on a hill to our left which some of our men were assailing and which they carried a few minutes later. . . . When the men got their wind we charged again and carried the second line of intrenchments with a rush. Swinging to the left, we thus drove the Spaniards over the brow of the chain of hills fronting Santiago. . . . Word was sent me to hold the line at all hazards, and that night we dug a line of intrenchments across our front, using the captured Spanish intrenching-tools. We had nothing to eat except what we captured from the Spaniards; but their dinner had fortunately been cooked, and we ate theirs with a relish, having been fighting all day."

That is the picture of the now historic charge up San Juan heights, drawn by one of the heroes in the lead; it was the Rough Riders' great opportunity, and gallantly did they improve it. Right well has Clinton Scollard tuned their rush to rhyme: —

> "Ay, they fought, let their blood attest! —
> The blood of their comrades gone;
> Fought their bravest and fought their best
> As when, like a wave, in their zealous zest
> They swept and surged o'er the sanguine crest
> Of the heights of San Juan."

But, with equal valor, the less heralded but fully as determined regulars flung themselves into the charge. Up the slopes and over the hills they swept; officers and men dropped beneath the deadly fire of ambushed sharpshooters and protected trench-men; at the ford, beneath the trees, and on the slopes they fell, but still the shirt-sleeved line pressed on. Mingling with the Rough Riders of the First Volunteer Cavalry, the black troopers of the Tenth charged with them the first of the fortified hills; crawling, running, charging, firing, the men from five regular infantry regiments indistinguishably mingled dashed, pell-mell, against Fort San Juan on the second hill, capturing the enemy's colors, sending the Spanish defenders scurrying to cover, and moving with that unconsciousness of disciplined heroism which led their commander General Kent, to say, "The bloody fighting of my brave command cannot be adequately described in words." Therefore, while, as Mr. Barnes says,

> "There's always a cheer for the volunteer,
>   There's ever a welcoming host,
> The wide land stretches a greeting hand —
>   Glad hail from the hill to the coast!
> There's none but will vaunt the deeds he's done!
>   Let us praise them and pledge him high!"

let us always gratefully remember the regulars, white and black. For, to quote again from Barnes's verse,

> "Who rushed the lines on the San Juan hill?
>   Who at Caney fought alone?
> The enlisted regular fighting man —
>   The soldier — bred to the bone!
> Who bore the big brunt of the battle front?
>   Should we speak it below a breath?
> The enlisted regular fighting man,
>   Who cheered as he charged to the death!"

THE RESERVES WAITING FOR ORDERS.
("We were to go in the moment they wavered and they didn't waver.")

And down under the hill, chafing at the discipline that necessarily kept him and his men in reserve for possible emergencies, the fighting major of the Second Cavalry gave just one grumble as the fight concluded: —

"We were to go in, boys, the moment they wavered," he complained; "but they didn't waver worth a cent, and so you've all missed being in the greatest charge that our army has ever made."

It was a great charge, indeed, even though it was not the theatrical onset of uniformed platoons with lowered bayonets and in serried ranks. That unbroken, unyielding advance up an intrenched hill, in the face of Spanish Mausers and with men dropping right and left, will be ever famous, ever historic; for the brave onrush of unfaltering, undismayed heroes in the face of certain death has glorified every such display of courage from Bunker Hill and Balaklava to Dargai Ridge and San Juan. It is such a deed, especially, as sets the Anglo-Saxon pulse a-tingle, making one forget nationality for a time and exclaim with the enthusiastic English captain, detailed for neutral observation, as he watched the assault on San Juan, "Boys, the victory is *ours!* the victory is *ours!*"

CHAPTER XI

HOW THEY SURPRISED THE GOVERNOR OF GUAM

THE third terrace in the three great upward steps from Siboney to Santiago was won, and the tired heroes of the regular and volunteer army of the United States, fighting through the night of July first to hold back the baffled and defeated Spaniards, rested a moment to "get their wind," as Colonel Roosevelt puts it, for the final assault upon the beleaguered town. As they rest thus in dog-tent and wickyup, or under the canopy of the changeful Cuban skies, we will turn for a moment to those parallel happenings which, in mid-Pacific and on the far-off Asiatic coast, were inevitably pushing the United States into the still unsettled problem of world-ruling. For the great republic seemed irresistibly forced to become a world-power in spite of itself.

When the news of Dewey's wonderful May-day achievement in Manila Bay was flashed under the ocean and across the continent from Hong Kong to Washington, at once the government hastened to despatch to the Philippines naval and military aid. Dewey was made a rear-admiral, and, on the eleventh of May General Wesley Merritt, a soldier of tried experience and ability, was ordered to Asiatic waters as governor-general of the Philippines.

On the twenty-fifth of May the first Manila military expedition sailed out from the harbor of San Francisco. It comprised the first division of the army assigned for duty in the Philippines — twenty-five hundred men with a year's supplies and a cargo of ammunition and naval stores, embarked in three transports; the troops were under the command of General Anderson, and were convoyed by the cruiser *Charleston*, commanded by Captain Glass.

The day after leaving Honolulu, where the expedition touched for ice and coal, Captain Glass opened his sealed instructions, according to orders, and there, for the first time, read that he was to stop on his way to Manila and capture the Spanish island of Guam.

The orders were "wigwagged" by signal to the troops on the transports, and at once officers and

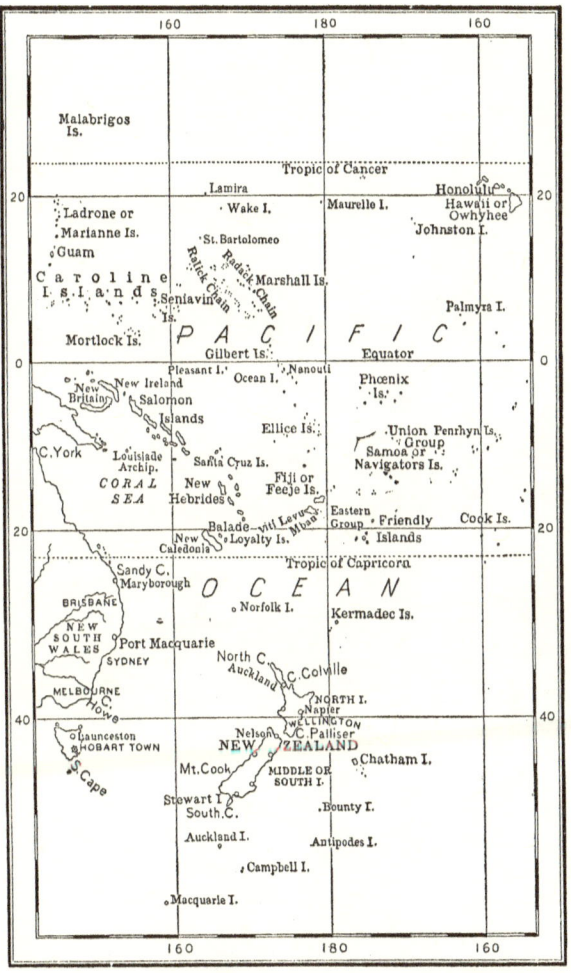

WHERE GUAM IS.

(Map showing position of Ladrone Islands in Pacific Ocean.)

men asked one another, "Where under the sun is Guam?" Scarcely one of all those twenty-five hundred men knew there was such a place. Do you?

Open your atlas at the map of Oceanica — that vast archipelago of Pacific islands lying between Asia and America. In that section of Oceanica known as Micronesia, west from Hawaii and east of Hong Kong, you will see a little group of islands labelled Mariana or Ladrone islands. There are fifteen islands in the group, and, of the fifteen, the largest and most southerly is Guahan or Guam.

When in the spring of 1521 that great navigator, Ferdinand Magellan, was cruising around the globe, he took the Ladrones on his way to the Philippines — as other navigators and conquerors have done since his day. He, too, landed on Guam and, because of the odd-looking sails on the odd-looking crafts of the islanders, he called them the "Islands of the Lateen Sails." But his sailors had certain experiences with the natives that gave them so poor an opinion of the place that forthwith they christened the group "Islas de las Ladrones" — the Islands of the Thieves. Later, when Spain had been misruling the islands for a hundred and forty years, the group was given the higher-toned name of Maria Anna, wife of the king of Spain then on the throne, and they were known to Spain as the Mariana Islands. But first names "stick," you know, and this group of Pacific islands, halfway between Honolulu and Hong Kong, are still best known by the nickname Magellan's sailors gave them — the Ladrone Islands, or Islands of the Thieves.

For nearly three hundred years Spain has held these fertile, lazy-life Pacific islands, using them in the usual Spanish way, crushing out all independence and enterprise, until with all their productive possibilities they became an expense rather than an income to Spain. So, as they happened to be a convenient midway station, and as Spain's methods and possession were equally in disfavor in the United States, Captain Glass's orders were to possess himself of the Ladrone Islands in behalf of the United States, and to make its Spanish officials and soldiers prisoners of war.

This he proceeded to do at once, and on the morning of Monday, the twentieth of June, the cruiser and the three transports rounded Apepas Island and the palisade-like cliffs of Point Orote, and sailed into the bay of San Luis d'Apra, the chief harbor of the island of Guam. A few miles up the coast was Agana, the capital. The abandoned fort at the point offered neither welcome nor opposition, and the bombardment of Fort Santa Cruz farther in shore brought no response from the silent Spanish guns.

Soon, however, the boats of the captain of the port and of the health officer, each flying the Spanish flag, pulled off to the fleet and boarded the cruiser. With them came an interpreter, a young Spanish-American, Barcelona-born, but made American by residence and naturalization in Chicago.

But Captain Glass of the *Charleston* needed no interpreter. He could talk to the Dons in the Dons' own tongue.

"Your pardon, Captain," said the captain of the port, "but if we might borrow the powder, we would gladly return your salute. Pray, Señor Captain, do not think us discourteous with our silent gun, but so few fleets honor us that we are not accustomed to receive salutes, and have no powder, if we would. We trust your health and the health of the fleet are good, and we beg to assure you, Señor Captain, that if we may but borrow the powder for the two old guns ashore at the port, it will honor us to be permitted to return your salute."

"Salute!" exclaimed Captain Glass. "I fired no salute. Do you not know, sir, the difference

"THE SILENT GUN."
("Salute, sir! I fired no salute," said Captain Glass.)

between a salute and shotted guns? Understand me, sir: the United States is at war with Spain; my salute, as you call it, was a bombardment; and you, gentlemen, must consider yourselves prisoners of war."

It was a very surprised and agitated brace of Spanish officials that heard this astounding information on the deck of the *Charleston*. For it proved to be a fact that, so dilatory are the actions of Spain, the officials and garrison at Guam had not yet been notified of the outbreak of hostilities nor the existence of war.

So Captain Glass let them off on parole for the day, with the understanding that they were to notify the governor of Guam at his capital of Agana that an American fleet was in the harbor and that the captain would be pleased to see the governor at once.

Lieutenant-Colonel Don José Marina de Vega, governor of Guam, was as much surprised as his subordinates; but Spanish official etiquette never yields to surprise.

That very evening came Captain Duarte, the secretary of the governor, to Captain Glass on the *Charleston*. He bore the "thousand welcomes" of his Excellency the governor of Guam to the "valiant American captain," but had the honor to inform him that the military law of Spain would not permit the governor of Guam to set foot on a foreign ship of war. "Would the honorable and valiant American captain do his Excellency the honor of waiting upon him in person in the morning?"

Now Captain Glass was in haste to be on the way to Manila, and America never permits punctilious etiquette to interfere with business.

"All right, sir," Captain Glass said to the secretary. "Tell the governor I'll see him in the morning, or send some one to see him."

When morning came, the captain decided to meet etiquette with etiquette. If the governor of Guam stood on ceremony, so would the captain of the *Charleston*. So he sent ashore as his representative the chief navigator of the *Charleston*, with an ensign and four men.

The guns of the *Charleston* covered the visitors, and commanded the landing at the port.

His Excellency the governor of Guam stood in state at the landing-place in the little village of Piti, with his secretary, the captain of the port, and the health officer, as reception committee. The chief navigator of the *Charleston* presented the communication from Captain Glass, which was, in effect, a summons to surrender unconditionally within thirty minutes, and significantly pointed to the fleet as the best reason for an affirmative answer.

"And, sir," added the chief navigator, "I call your attention to these facts in order that you may not make any hasty or ill-conditioned reply to the note of my commandant."

The Spaniards themselves have a proverb: "There is no making a good cloak of bad cloth." His Excellency the governor of Guam had struck

THE U.S. CRUISER CHARLESTON.
(Which convoyed the transports to Manila and, with its salute that was no salute, surprised the governor of Guam.)

a mighty bad piece of cloth for a Spanish cloak. But all Spaniards are philosophical, so he concluded to make a virtue of necessity, and not return an "ill-conditioned reply." He was moved to this conclusion all the stronger as, looking down the harbor, he saw the steam launch of the *Charleston* towing a string of boats filled with marines and soldiers from the fleet.

Twenty-nine minutes of the thirty passed. Then his Excellency the governor of Guam came from his office with a letter.

"It is my reply to your commandant, Señor Lieutenant," he said.

"I represent him, sir," replied the chief navigator, putting up the watch on which he had been checking off the thirty minutes, and breaking the seal of the letter.

It was the "unconditional surrender" demanded.

"In the absence of any notification from my government concerning the relations of war between the United States and Spain," said the governor in his letter, "and without any means of defence or the possibility of defence in the face of such a large opposing force, I feel compelled, in the interests of humanity and to save life, to make a complete surrender of all under my jurisdiction."

Thus was Guam captured. The governor and his associates, the officers and men of his "regular army," sixty in all, were sent aboard the fleet as prisoners of war; the stars and stripes rose over

Fort Santa Cruz, the guns boomed a salute, the bands played, the soldiers and sailors cheered, and the Ladrone Islands became an American possession by lawful conquest, while the young Spanish-American who had offered his services as interpreter was named by Captain Glass governor-general of Guam.

His Excellency Don Marina de Vega, late governor of Guam, did not recover from his surprise until he was well on his way to Manila, a prisoner of war. For then he knew that the fleet had come, not to capture Guam, but to reënforce Manila. When he reached that far-off Philippine port his surprise was renewed. For there, before the old walled capital of Spain's Asiatic colonies, floated a victorious American fleet of warships. In and about the harbor lay the charred remains of the splendid Spanish fleet upon which every Spanish official in Asiatic waters had depended for security and defence against the enemies of Spain. Above the Spanish arsenal at Cavité floated the stars and stripes, while the embattled rock of Corregidor, which frowns above the entrance to Manila Harbor, no longer displayed the golden standard of Spain. It is no wonder that his Excellency the ex-governor of Guam, who had

IN PHILIPPINE WATERS.
(*Olympia* and *Raleigh* off the coast of Luzon.)

laid his head upon the table and wept in chagrin and despair when forced to surrender his little Ladrone archipelago, — specks only on the map of the Pacific, — should have felt even more bitterly the sting of defeat as he glanced on the dismantled outworks of Manila, the blockading Yankee fleet swinging across the beautiful bay, and the vanguard of the Yankee army of possession, whose prisoner of war he was, coming to the conquest and occupation of the great and rich island group which his forefathers, hundreds of years before, had seized and held for Spain.

Humanity alone held back the Yankee invaders

of those far-off islands from completing the work begun by Dewey on the first of May. It would have been better had it been thus settled at once. For about the city of Manila swarmed the rebellious Filipinos, rearoused to revolt against the Spaniards by the coming of the Americans and the victory over the Spanish fleet. One after another, the military expeditions sailed across the sea from America, until, at last, there were in Philippine waters and before the walls of Manila, besides the reënforced fleet of battleships, sixteen thousand American soldiers, both regulars and volunteers.

Other nations would have completed the business at once. But to Americans the insurgent Filipinos seemed men fighting for independence, and toward all such, half-civilized though they were, the sentiment of brotherhood went out from all America, even though those in authority doubted how far it was safe to trust the proffered alliance of these island rebels.

But Dewey had not sailed to Manila to join hands with the Filipinos; Merritt and his men had not gone over the sea to back up Aguinaldo's shadowy claims. They were in Manila Bay to break the power of Spain, and to guard the interests which, by victory, had become American.

"Only reluctance to cause needless loss of life and property," says President McKinley, "prevented the early storming and capture of the city, and therewith the absolute military occupancy of the whole group. The insurgents, meanwhile, had resumed the active hostilities suspended by the uncompleted truce of December, 1897. Their forces invested Manila from the northern and eastern sides, but were constrained by Admiral Dewey and General Merritt from attempting an assault. It was fitting that whatever was to be done in the way of decisive operations in that quarter should be accomplished by the strong arm of the United States alone. Obeying the stern precept of war which enjoins the overcoming of the adversary and the extinction of his power wherever assailable as the speedy and sure means to win a peace, divided victory was not permissible, for no partition of the rights and responsibilities attending the enforcement of a just and advantageous peace could be thought of."

"A partition of rights and responsibilities," if such division were to come about, seemed desired by other than the rebel Filipinos. Scarcely had the smoke of Dewey's May-day guns blown away when, from every quarter, came the swift-sailing warships of European and foreign powers, ostensibly to protect national interests, but really to watch Dewey and each other as well.

France and Germany, England and Japan, sent their cruisers into Manila Bay — the first two in a critical, the last two in a friendly, spirit. It seemed unfortunate that Germany, especially — a nation whose interests in so many ways run side by side with those of America, whose blood courses in so many American veins, who have equal share with England and America in what the Emperor of Germany so rightly calls "the deeds of our great common race," and whose friendly hand-clasp has even been desired and welcomed by the great republic, should have, through her naval representative, ranged herself in apparent though unofficial hostility against America's power in Manila Bay.

But America's power in Manila Bay was intrusted to one who would countenance no foreign interference in support of Spain's ruined power nor in the instigation of unacknowledged insurgent resistance. So when by one and another significant act the German warships sought to invade the rights and interfere with the duties of the victorious Americans, as recognized by the rules of war, Admiral Dewey — for he was rear-admiral now, and the blue pennant with the two stars streamed from the *Olympia's* mainmast — bided his time.

He said little, for the admiral was a man of few words, as are all doers of great deeds. Only once in his dry way did he observe to the German flag-lieutenant: "One might almost think your ships were blockading Manila, and not mine."

But when at last one of the German cruisers — there were six of them at Manila by this time — began to lay down the law to the Filipinos, and another one tried to run the American blockade and, with all lights out, creep up to an anchorage nearer to Manila, while yet another, violating neutrality, landed provisions at Manila, Admiral Dewey felt that the climax had been reached.

He summoned his flag-lieutenant.

"Mr. Brumby," he said, in the calm, even tone that was a part of the Dewey firmness of character, "I wish you to take the barge and go over to the German flagship. Give Admiral von Diederich my compliments, and say that I wish to call his attention to the fact that the vessels of his squadron have shown an extraordinary disregard of the usual courtesies of naval intercourse, and that, finally, one of them has committed a gross breach of neutrality in landing provisions in Manila, a port which I am blockading."

"Ay, ay, sir," responded the flag-lieutenant, glad of this opportunity to speak the admiral's mind and voice the indignation of the fleet.

The admiral paused as the flag-lieutenant saluted and turned to go. Then, as if it were an afterthought, when it was in fact the postscript to the official communication — a postscript in which was centred all the indignation, determination, and pluck of the aroused admiral, Dewey called after his departing flag-lieutenant in a voice louder and more emphatic than was his wont: —

"And, Brumby," he said, in words that all the nation applauded when the "postscript" was reported across the sea, "you may tell Admiral von Diederich that if he wants a fight, he can have it right now."

Admiral von Diederich, of course, "declined the honor"; he had no desire or authority to risk conclusions with the American fleet. He hastened to assure Admiral Dewey that he was not aware of the misdoings of his captains and that they "should not occur again."

They did not. The firm stand of our victorious

admiral which could overawe troublesome Filipinos and hold the Spaniards in check had its influence also upon the arrogance of German naval authority, and sternly repressed what Germany now describes as "Admiral von Diederich's grave want of tact"; so there was never any need for Admiral Dewey to repeat his message to the chief of the German fleet.

Thus, in two hemispheres, American affairs drew on toward a climax. For while Admiral Dewey "held the whip handle" before the walls of Manila, and the detachments of American soldiers, one after another, arrived on the big transports from over sea to back up his authority; while Spain, in desperation, gathered together her last fleet of warships to send them eastward through the Suez Canal to Dewey's destruction, and Commodore Watson, a veteran of the American navy, was ordered to collect a fleet of warships for a possible descent on the coast of Spain, the gallant Fifth Army Corps, victorious in Cuba, occupied the conquered trenches of El Caney and San Juan, and drawing its cordon closer about the beleaguered city prepared for its final descent in assault from its dog-tents and its wicky-ups spread over the intrenched hills that looked down upon Santiago.

CHAPTER XII

HOW THE SPANISH ADMIRAL MADE A DASH FOR LIBERTY

ADMIRAL SCHLEY.

UPON the hills looking down on Santiago lay the advance of the American army. A victory, dearly bought at the cost of sixteen hundred dead and wounded men, had given that army the complete investment of Santiago on the north and east, while about their trenches and within the beleaguered town thousands of Spaniards lay dead or wounded, victims of their own brave persistency.

But though the heights were won and Santiago was before them, the position of the victors was most precarious. Lying in an exposed position, within range and rifle-shot of Spanish outposts and defences, with a strongly intrenched and valiant foe before them and reënforcements for the Spaniards nearing the town, with a lamentable lack of field artillery and no siege-guns at hand, with their ammunition low and their base of supplies far in the rear, with few intrenching-tools and no

TRENCH-MAKING BEFORE SANTIAGO.
(Soldiers digging trenches with plates and knives.)

trenches dug that would shield them from Spanish attack, — which by daylight might be terrible in its intensity and fatal in its effects, — soaked with the heavy rains and hungry from lack of food, it would not be strange if the first flush of triumph should fade into the gloom of doubt and that the officers, responsible for the safety and lives of their men, should question the wisdom of retaining the advanced position on the heights, and should even urge upon the commanding general a withdrawal to a safer position back of the heights and nearer their base of supplies.

There was good reason for this from a military point of view; for the responsibility of the advanced position was great, and, as General Shafter says, "the man who can carry lightly his responsibility for the lives of thousands of men is not fit to command;" but neither officers nor men — not even those most in danger or those exposed to a possibly destructive Spanish fire — had the wish to see a backward movement that the world would call a retreat.

Intrenching on the hill as best they could with their scant supply of tools, threatened again and again with Spanish sortie and attack, the American advance on the heights pluckily held their own; the decision to withdraw was not taken; instead, General Shafter determined to remain where he was and push the siege with vigor. So as a bold move toward the end, he decided that on the morning of Sunday, the third of July, he would demand the unconditional surrender of the city of Santiago and the Spanish army defending it.

But on the morning of Sunday, the third of

July, 1898, another factor entered into the war-filled chapter of Santiago's story that few men anticipated, though all men deemed it possible.

Steadily about the beleaguered city drew the American army; stretched in a merciless cordon about the entrance to the narrow-necked harbor

CAMP OF THE AMERICAN ADVANCE.
("The American advance on the heights pluckily held their own.")

floated the ships of the American blockaders; the army and navy of Spain at Santiago alike were doomed unless some desperate sortie succeeded on the land, or a mad dash for liberty freed the Spanish ships.

To Admiral Cervera, commanding the fine Spanish fleet of cruisers and destroyers at Santiago, there came orders from Madrid and Havana to break away from Santiago, run the American blockade, and at all risks carry his squadron to the assistance of Havana or the safety of some non-blockaded port.

Admiral Cervera knew better than his superiors the folly of such an order; but a sailor's first duty is, like a soldier's, to obey orders, and he proceeded to make ready for his dash to liberty or death.

The guns of the fleet which had been sent on shore to aid the besieged city were reshipped; the sailors who were helping in the defence of the town were recalled, and the quiet of a Sunday morning was selected for the desperate attempt, because, on Sunday morning, the ships of every navy are occupied with the details of dress review, inspection, and church services, and the thoughts of officers and crews are not fixed on fighting.

But the discipline on the ships of Admiral Sampson's fleet was like clockwork in its regularity and precision. There are warships on which, though every man is drilled to his duty and knows his place, those are precisely the things he forgets or blunders over when the critical moment of test arrives. But it was not so in Admiral Sampson's squadron. Five weeks of watchful blockading had made every man "letter-perfect" in his part, and the thing they remembered best was the admiral's simple but explicit order: "If the enemy tries to escape, the ships must close and engage as soon as possible, and endeavor to sink his vessels or force them to run ashore."

As the sun sprang above the horizon with true tropical velocity and dispelled the low-hanging curtain of mist on that warm Sunday morning of July 3, it showed the warships riding at their several stations in a broken half-circle in front of Santiago harbor. There rode in the centre, looking straight into the narrow entrance, the *Iowa* of Captain Evans; east of her lay the famous *Oregon* of Captain Clark and the *Indiana* of Captain Taylor; west of Captain Evans were the *Texas* of Captain Philip and the *Brooklyn* of Captain Cook, flying the pennant of Commodore Schley, second in command of the fleet. On the horns of the half-circle and closer inshore rode the two little auxiliaries, gunboats made over from yachts, the *Vixen* on the western end, commanded by Lieutenant Sharp, and, at the eastern end, the *Gloucester* in charge of the same Lieutenant-commander Wainwright who had been executive officer of the *Maine* that fatal February night in Havana harbor.

Scarcely was the sun well up when the other vessels of the blockading squadron were steaming off on various errands.

THE INNER HARBOR OF SANTIAGO.

"Disregard movements of the commander-in-chief," read the admiral's signal from the masthead of the flagship *New York*, as, accompanied by the torpedo boat *Ericsson*, she sailed to the eastward for a conference at Siboney between the admiral and General Shafter as to the conduct of a joint campaign.

"If I leave I'm sure something will happen,"

the admiral had said, dreading to leave his post at a critical time. But the conference was a necessity; and even though, so long as the senior officer was not actually out of signal distance, the real responsibility of command was not shifted, still he knew that he had left a vigilant second in charge in the person of Commodore Schley.

So off to Siboney the admiral sailed early that Sunday morning, while the cruiser *Massachusetts* with the destroyers *Suwanee* and *Vesuvius* had also withdrawn from the squadron and gone to Guantanamo for coal.

The sun rose higher; the warm July morning grew hotter; the awnings were spread on the warships, and the crew in their "Sunday-go-to-meeting rig" were piped to "general muster"; over the water, from the *Texas*, came the bugle-call to church, and the bells of the fleet chimed musically in. It was a quiet, restful summer Sunday morning at sea; but, nevertheless, the watchers and lookouts were all at their proper posts, discipline was not relaxed, and on more than one warship the signal of danger was strung ready to be "broken out" at the first sign of hostile action.

Inspection had already begun on the *Iowa* when, from the bridge, came a shout.

A DASH FOR LIBERTY

"The fleet's coming out!" rang the warning.

Up flew the ready signal to stream out from the *Iowa's* yard: "The enemy is escaping to the westward!" while from the *Iowa's* forward bridge the six-pounder boomed its noisy warning.

On the other ships, also, vigilant eyes had sighted danger. The navigator on the forward bridge of the *Brooklyn* dropped the long glass through which he had descried a moving column of smoke behind the harbor hill, and caught up the megaphone.

"After-bridge, there!" he shouted; "report to the commodore and the captain that the enemy's ships are coming out!"

It was half-past nine on Sunday morning; just the time when the "folks at home" were thinking of getting ready for church. Signals flew; men scattered to their stations; officers took their posts, and all the ships and auxiliaries "cleared for action."

As the signals fluttered out, the fleet was heading inshore, according to the admiral's instructions, so as to be able to lose no time in turning if the enemy should run out. For the admiral had every point in sea-strategy and sea-action at his fingers' ends. And the signals told the truth. The enemy's fleet was indeed coming out.

Nerved to his desperate duty, Admiral Cervera had selected the time when the blockading squadron had been weakened by the withdrawal of five of its vessels — two cruisers and three smaller boats; he had selected church time on Sunday morning, when he imagined the Yankee tars would be least prepared for fighting; he had his guns all ready and his decks cleared for action; he had arranged with the forts and shore batteries to support his movements with a terrific fire, and he had directed his gunners to concentrate their fire upon the *Brooklyn*, so as to cripple or destroy her, as she was the fastest sailer in the American fleet.

Then, creeping down the channel, past the sunken *Merrimac* just showing her smoke-stack above the water, past the batteries that were ready to help in the escape, the Spanish squadron steamed toward the sea, the admiral's flagship leading. Six hundred yards apart, came the four big and beautiful cruisers of the Spanish fleet; twelve hundred yards behind the cruisers the two torpedo boats brought up the rear. Her opposing forces were seven to six — one in favor of the Americans; but the Spanish fleet had three armored cruisers where the Americans had but one, and upon that one they were directed to concentrate their fire.

Now "that one" was the armored cruiser *Brooklyn*, the responsible leader of the depleted fleet, and on its quarterdeck was Winfield Scott Schley, commodore and senior officer in that famous fight.

WHERE CERVERA RAN OUT.

(Entrance to Santiago harbor. Morro on the height to the right. The Spanish fleet came out to the left of Morro and turned to the west — the left.)

Down the channel, one by one, the Spanish warships steamed, around the western point they swung, and then, with their boilers worked to the highest, open draught and all steam on, with their port guns thundering defiance and every available shore battery cannonading in support, the *Maria Teresa* and the *Vizcaya*, the *Colon* and the *Oquendo*, four as fine cruisers as were afloat, with the deadly torpedo boats *Furor* and *Pluton* bringing up the rear, sprang out of Santiago harbor and headed for the westward in one mad dash for liberty. It was as brave and bold, as desperate and defiant, a forlorn hope as may be found in all the long story of Spain upon the seas, since first Hamilcar, grandfather of the great Hannibal, with Carthaginians and Spaniards laid his mighty fleet upon the Sicilian coast. And even like Hamilcar did Cervera come to grief.

There was no delay on the part of the American squadron in answering the Spaniards' challenge, and darting to head off the foe. Even as a crowd of alert and watchful boys spring to head off their opponents on a break from "goal," or when a straining football team leaps to tackle or stop its rival eleven in their wild rush down the field, so did the American warships fling themselves upon their Spanish foemen.

"Signal the fleet to clear ship!" the commodore commanded. "Have your rapid-fire guns ready for those fellows, Captain Cook. Ensign McCauley, signal the fleet to close in."

Straight into the mouth of the harbor, forcing draughts and increasing speed, the Americans dashed, the commodore on the *Brooklyn* farthest to the west. Then, as the Spaniards turned sharply to the westward, the Americans turned westward as well, and in parallel lines burst into chase like hounds upon the trail.

"The *Brooklyn*," said Commodore Schley in his report to the admiral, "being thus directly in the route taken by the Spanish squadron, was exposed, possibly for ten minutes, to the gun fire of three of the Spanish ships and the west battery; but the vessels of the entire squadron, closing in rapidly, soon diverted this fire, and did magnificent work at close range."

This "closing in" was done by perfect seamanship as well as perfect marksmanship; for as the other cruisers saw the peril of the *Brooklyn* they rushed to her aid, bunching and closing in once again like trained football players. The great *Oregon*, like "the bulldog of the seas" it had been called, rushed "like a thunder-bolt," the foam breaking high before her bows; straight in between the *Texas* and the *Iowa* she dashed, and held her fire as she passed the *Iowa;* but the instant she drew ahead she poured her fire upon the Spanish fleet with so close a calculation that her after-guns blazed out across the forecastle of the *Iowa*.

"Put your helm hard aport," said Commodore Schley, as the *Vizcaya* left the Spanish line and came straight at the *Brooklyn*. Around came the helm and around swung the big cruiser, not away from, but toward, the puzzled enemy, her port guns belching five-inch, six-inch, and eight-inch projectiles. Twenty of these in all sent their fatal shot plunging into the *Vizcaya* and the *Maria Teresa;* then, turning again, the *Brooklyn* let go her starboard battery, completely "rattling" the Spaniards who had singled her out for destruction.

"Tell the men to fire deliberately and make every shot tell," said the commodore. And every man in all the fleet, from the captain on the bridge to the stoker in the furnace-room, did his "level best," realizing that he had a share in the greatest fight of his life.

Now to starboard and now to port the helms of the warships swung, as, right upon the heels of the fleeing Spaniards they sprang in fierce assault. Unable to repel or to resist the merciless American fire, their own guns wrongly set or served by inefficient and irresponsible gunners, doomed, as they saw, to swift and sure defeat, the Spanish captains thought, first, only of escape, and then only of how to die without surrender.

A DASH FOR LIBERTY

Westward still along the coast they flew, — their guns noisy but harmless, — the American warships raking them with a terrible and telling fire of shot and shell. One after another they burst into flame, now fore and now aft, and, still pursued by the relentless Americans, at last, in sheer desperation, they steered straight inshore to beach and burn in wreck.

Craftiest of all the Spanish fleet, the *Colon* (or *Columbus*), third in the line, dropped behind the other Spanish vessels, and as the chase forged ahead drew herself almost out of range, and escaped the first fierce fire of the American ships. Under her protecting bulk ran the torpedo destroyers *Furor* and *Pluton;* but the *Colon*, in the vain belief that safety and even escape lay in her instant flight, suddenly sprang away from the destroyers, and with a mighty spurt outdistanced the American fleet, with a six-mile lead.

Left to themselves, the destroyers *Furor* and *Pluton* looked for other cover, and while one steamed ahead to shield itself behind one of the armored cruisers, the *Pluton*, under the fire of the shore batteries, sought to crawl back into the harbor.

But an avenger was on her track. Wainwright,

the last man excepting its commander to leave the sinking *Maine*, was, as you remember, commander of the *Gloucester*, the eastern picket of the blockading fleet. As the Spaniards left the harbor, Wainwright drove the little *Gloucester*— an unprotected, converted steam pleasure yacht — straight at the big *Oquendo*, although upon him bore the full fury of the guns of Morro Castle. Paying no attention to the fusilade from shore, the *Gloucester* plumped her six-pounders into the *Oquendo*, who, suspecting herself attacked by a torpedo boat, turned her batteries upon the yacht. Just then, however, the *Gloucester* caught sight of the low-lying *Furor* and *Pluton*, sneaking off for shelter and escape, and judging these to be about her size, drew off from the now flying *Oquendo*, and devoted herself to the fast-sailing destroyers, either one of which "outclassed" her in speed and armament, but not, it would seem, in discipline and marksmanship.

For an instant the battle raged about and above these three small craft. The *Oquendo* and the *Maria Teresa*, with the shore batteries, sought at first to support the destroyers, while the *Iowa*, the *Indiana*, and the *Oregon* backed up the plucky *Gloucester*. The fight was brief but fierce. Over

WAINWRIGHT ON THE GLOUCESTER.

("The *Maine* is avenged!" he is reported to have said, sternly and solemnly.)

A DASH FOR LIBERTY 239

the *Gloucester's* deck a great shell cut the air and, fatally directed, fell plump in the middle of the destroyer *Pluton*, which, riddled already by the *Gloucester's* six-pounders, sank in an instant — even more quickly than the *Maine* had gone down. Then the big ships turned their attention upon each other, while the *Gloucester*, darting ahead, turned back the *Furor* from trying to shield herself behind the *Oquendo*, and plunging into her a deadly fire at close range, with the occasional assistance of the *Indiana*, drove her in shore, where she broke on a reef and sank in the breaking surf.

Whereupon the gallant Wainwright, even though he may have said sternly and solemnly as is reported, "The *Maine* is avenged!" turned to the humane work of rescuing the men of the wrecked destroyers, which, twenty minutes after they had left the harbor of Santiago, were broken and sunken hulks.

Even as the *Gloucester* was finishing off the *Furor*, down the coast and past the plucky little fighter, came rushing the flagship *New York*. When off Altares, seven miles to the eastward, she had seen the signs of battle. At once she came about and running up the quite unnecessary signal, "Close in toward harbor entrance and attack vessels," sailed in on the heels of the chase.

Straight across the harbor's mouth, unheeding the plunging fire of the shore batteries directed full upon her, she raced, scarce noticing the shells that exploded above and around her.

"Let us go on — on, after the enemy," the admiral exclaimed again and again, and on and on the flagship forged ahead.

As she passed the *Gloucester*, she threw some shells at the *Furor*, as a naval "pat on the back" for the yacht; but "the *Gloucester*," as Captain Chadwick of the *New York* reported, "proved herself so capable that the ship stood on."

But as the flagship passed the *Gloucester* the crew of the *New York* sprang to the forecastle deck, and led by their captain cheered the plucky little yacht to the echo. Then she dashed on to be in at the death.

The "death" came even before the flagship could come up. One after the other the Spanish cruisers, swept by flame, ran ashore and dropped their flags in surrender. First to succumb, the *Maria Teresa*, at 10.15, beached in the surf six miles from the harbor she had cleared; fifteen minutes later the *Oquendo* ran ashore, half a mile beyond the *Teresa;* then the *Vizcaya*, the admiral's flagship, after one last bold dash to ram her chief rival, the *Brooklyn*, was driven ashore fifteen miles from Santiago and struck her colors at 11.15; and Wainwright of the *Gloucester*, the survivor of the *Maine*, by a sort of poetic justice, rescued the

U. S. CRUISER BROOKLYN.

(Commodore Schley's flagship, which led the sea-fight of July 3.)

sinking Spanish admiral Cervera from the wreck of his flagship and received his surrender on board the deck of the *Gloucester*.

No need to question how or by whom this victory was won. There was honor enough for all to have a share, from admiral to ensign, from engineer to stoker. Each had done his part. The noble fleet of Spain was cornered, conquered, destroyed.

But the fleeing *Colon*, springing from that line of death in one last fierce dash for life, sped on up the coast with the *Brooklyn* and the *Oregon*, the *Texas*, the little *Vixen*, and finally the flagship *New York*, in full chase.

On past the beached and burning cruisers of Spain (their drowning crews now being rescued by the men who had hammered them in fight) the American flagship sped and rounded up the chase just as, offshore, fifty miles from Santiago, the *Colon*, last of Cervera's fleet, lowered her flag and surrendered to the *Brooklyn*.

Then, when Spanish bad faith, after this surrender, would have destroyed and sunk the *Colon* in deep water, the *New York* laid her nose against the sinking cruiser and actually "bunted" her ashore, where she grounded in shoal water.

Six hundred men killed, two thousand taken prisoners, four cruisers and two torpedo-boat destroyers driven ashore in wreck and surrender, — twelve million dollars' worth of naval property and Spain's only serviceable fleet wiped out at one blow, — that was the record of Spanish disaster! And the American record? One man killed and three wounded on the cruiser *Brooklyn*, which was struck twenty times by comparatively

A DASH FOR LIBERTY

harmless projectiles, two slight "strikes" of no importance against the *Iowa*, and that was all! Out of that terrible Spanish fire our fleet rode unharmed; in the midst of that destructive American fire the fleet of Spain went down in wreck and ruin. Do you wonder that men called it miraculous? Do you wonder that good Captain Philip of the *Texas*, impressed by the magnitude of the victory and the absolute freedom from injury, piped his crew to prayers even before the smoke of victory had died away, and standing among them with bared head, said solemnly: "Men, I want to make public acknowledgment here that I believe in God the Father. I want you all to lift your hats and, from your hearts, offer silent thanks to the Almighty."

And yet the miracle, under God's grace, was of man's own making. For it was the victory of right over injustice, of discipline over demoralization, of confidence over insecurity, of perfect training over inefficiency, of careful marksmanship over unskilful gunnery, of the men behind the guns over the men afraid of their guns.

"The race is not always to the swift nor the battle to the strong." But when the swift races with brain alert, and the strong fights with the strength of discipline, any other result than victory would indeed be a miracle.

That was why the fleet of Admiral Sampson, sailed according to his orders and led by Commodore Schley, smashed Cervera's fleet in its bold dash for liberty and achieved the wonderful victory of Sunday, July 3. As Admiral Sampson himself says of it: —

" The fleets that were opposed to each other on that Sunday morning were, as regards the numbers of the ships, about six to seven. Leaving out the torpedo destroyers and the *Gloucester*, which may be said not to have been fighting ships," — although we know how they did fight, — " the proportion was six to four. The fleet of the Spaniards were four beautiful ships. I think I am stating the case within bounds when I say that, barring their condition at that time, — which, of course, we did not all know, — they were, in many respects, all our imaginations had led us to suppose. We outnumbered them about three to one, but this is only another illustration of the fact that it is necessary to have a superior force to make sure of victory in any case."

CHAPTER XIII

WHY THEY CHEERED IN THE TRENCHES

EVEN had Admiral Sampson not seen the smoke and heard the sounds of conflict that sent him so swiftly to the right about on that famous Sunday morning in July, he would have found when he rode over the hills from Siboney to confer with General Shafter that the general had already taken the bull by the horns.

For that very Sunday morning, just as the Spanish fleet was steaming down the channel to escape or death, General Shafter, at half-past eight o'clock, sent this summons to General Toral, the Spanish commander in Santiago:—

"I have the honor to inform you that, unless you surrender, I shall be obliged to shell Santiago de Cuba. Please instruct the citizens of all foreign countries, and all women and children, that they should leave the city before 10 A.M. to-morrow."

Even while considering the question of withdrawal to a point nearer his base of supplies, the general was making ready to push the siege of Santiago. But even as the flag of truce bore this demand for surrender, there crept somehow into the trenches where the boys waited for orders the report that Admiral Cervera and his fleet had

BAMBOO BRIDGE OVER THE SAN JUAN RIVER.
(On the road to Santiago.)

escaped from Santiago harbor. It was depressing, but the boys said never a word.

Then at noon came the real news, joyfully sent from headquarters with the order: "Rush this information all around our lines at the front." And as it was rushed the boys all along the line, even to the trenches on the hills, went wild over the good news, for they knew, as did all the world, that the destruction of Spain's last available fleet finished the business in Cuba and must end the war. There was a regimental band, even at the front, and it played "The Star-Spangled Banner," and "There'll be a Hot Time in the Old Town To-night," until the puffed-out cheeks of the hungry musicians almost burst, from their energy, while the boys, careless of the insecurity of their trenches, leaped up and down with joy and cheered until they were hoarse, and all, "officers and men," said General Shafter, "though even without shelter tents and soaked for five days in the afternoon rains, all are happy."

But if the boys in the trenches, knowing that Cervera's overthrow would end the war, felt that it would end it at once, they did not know the methods of diplomatic "giving-in" nor the inbred "putting-off ways" of Spain.

At first, in reply to General Shafter's demand, the Spanish commander replied, "It is my duty to say to you that this city will not surrender;" then General Shafter, at the request of the foreign consuls in Santiago, and out of regard for the women and children, put off the threatened bombardment until July 5; then it was put off to send in the wounded Spanish officers; then to arrange for the exchange of the brave Hobson of the *Merrimac*, a prisoner in Santiago with his plucky crew; then to lend the Spanish general some of our own telegraph operators to communicate with Madrid; then to receive a proposition for evacuation; and so on, " backing and filling " and requesting and yielding (all in the interests of humanity), now breaking off the truce on the tenth of July, and on the eleventh putting it on again, while all the time the

IN THE TRENCHES.
("One shovel to a regiment.")

American soldiers lay in the trenches they had made when there was just " one shovel to a regiment," as one of the boys said; while fever crept into their systems and the calls for quinine grew more and more frequent; while the trenches broke down or washed apart under the heavy tropical rains, and beef and pork and hardtack even lost the taste they never had, and the tempting qualities that are only on the label, and while, all the time, the boys, anxious to close things up, chafed under delay and agreed with the impatient cowboy soldier who exclaimed, " Well! now we've got those Mexicans corralled, why don't we go in and brand 'em ? "

Ignorant, too, of the meaning of all this "backing and filling," and all the flags of truce and extensions of armistice, the soldier boys, with true American restlessness, disapproved of all this "chassezing" and "issuing extras," as they called the frequent conferences. They talked it over as American soldiers will, until one of the regulars, perplexed over the armistices and the delay, expressed himself to Mr. Davis, according to that enterprising correspondent's report: —

"Say, I can't make out this flag of truce gag. It reminds me of two kids in a street fight, stopping after every punch to ask the other feller if he's had enough. Why don't we keep at it until somebody gets hurted ? "

Somebody had got "hurted," but, like a brave

soldier, did not wish to give in until he could do so with honor.

So the flags of truce came and went, but the result of one of these journeys again set the trenches to cheering.

It was on the sixth of July that General Shafter proposed to General Toral an exchange of a Spanish lieutenant and seven men for Naval Constructor Hobson and his seven men, prisoners in Santiago.

Under a spreading ceiba, or great silk-cotton tree, the exchange of prisoners was arranged; and late in the afternoon of that same sixth of July, after he had been for six weeks a prisoner under fire in Santiago, the release came, and, as Mr. Davis graphically describes it, " with the rifle-pits behind him filled with thousands of the enemy, with the rifle-pits before him filled with thousands of his friends, Hobson and his seven comrades rode out into the welcoming arms of the American army and into their inheritance."

That inheritance was the one word "heroes!" and, as the first fruits, the trenches were alive with cheering men. The band struck up " The Star-Spangled Banner," cavalrymen and infantry uncovered in salute as the hero of the *Merrimac* rode by, and then, with a wild burst of welcoming and

A SILK-COTTON TREE.

(Under such a tree as this, the ceiba or silk-cotton tree, the negotiations for surrender took place.)

appreciative cheers, the men who, at the risk of their lives upon the blood spattered heights before Santiago, had so fought as to set him and his comrades free, waved hats and hands in frantic salute, and filled the air with the loud ringing response to the oft-repeated demand, "Now, boys, once more! Three cheers for Hobson!"

Still the flags of truce came and went; still the Spaniard protested and held out; still the American threatened and yielded another day. A conference between the army and navy resulted in an agreement for a joint attack from sea and shore; but the presence of so many non-combatants and friends of America in Santiago held off the attack day after day, while, through fear of it, hundreds and thousands of refugees streamed out of the besieged and starving city toward dismantled and over-crowded El Caney.

MULE TRAIN ON THE WAY TO RELIEVE THE SANTIAGO REFUGEES.

Finally the Spanish commander offered to evacuate Santiago and march away with his troops; but President McKinley was firm.

"We must have the city and the soldiers," he decided. "The surrender must be unconditional."

Then, as Spanish diplomacy failed, Spanish bluff

WHY THEY CHEERED IN THE TRENCHES 253

tried its hand. The long truce was suddenly ended at four o'clock on the afternoon of July 10; the men on both sides dropped into the shelter of their trenches or their ramparts, and hostile shots flew

THE CHURCH AT EL CANEY.
(Fortified by the Spaniards, won by the Americans, and used as a hospital for refugees.)

across the debated ground, while off Aguadores the fleet began to shell the city.

Then American generosity played its part. Next day, at noon, on the eleventh, the last gun was fired. For there had come from Washington a telegram stating that if the Spanish would surrender unconditionally, the United States government would agree to ship the soldiers home to Spain at its own expense.

Once more the white flags fluttered out, that this generous offer from a victorious foeman might be communicated to the Spanish general; once more the information was cabled to Madrid "for the consideration of Spain," and once more the boys in the trenches and under the hills waited for developments and swapped *buenas* with the Spanish boys, also waiting for developments. "One morning at 11.30 o'clock," says one of the officers, "the army was ordered into the rifle-pits. It was terribly hot in the trenches. We waited until 12.30, and still the opening gun was not heard. One man said that he had rather be shot than roast to death in that oven, and the men got out of the pits. In two or three minutes another regiment got out, and was seated on the ground in front. The Spaniards also got out, and there were the two armies, looking at each other."

Slowly the developments they were waiting for came. From the third of July, when the heights fronting Santiago had been so bravely won and the fleet of Cervera had been so marvellously destroyed, until the fifteenth of July, when Spaniard and American met under the spreading ceiba tree where they had arranged for the release of Hobson, Spaniard and American waited for the end they knew must speedily come.

"In my opinion this closes the war with Spain," General Shafter telegraphed to the President, when, after the government's generous offer to send home the Spanish troops, the Spanish general inquired if the offer included his entire command.

"The moment Admiral Cervera's fleet was destroyed," an observant English authority declared, "the war was practically at an end, unless Spain had elected to fight on to save the point of honor."

But whether the army or the navy was the chief factor in the final result, it is certain that for a few days the answer of the Spanish commander was delayed or given "in instalments" and it was uncertain whether or not Spain would, as the Englishman suggested, "fight on to save the point of honor."

Whatever was to be the result, the Yankee boys in the trenches were not to be caught napping.

"We kept right on working," says General Clark of the Second Massachusetts. "We had extended our lines until we reached a point where the foothills terminated. We moved down from the foothills on the morning of the twelfth of July. This was during the truce. We paid no attention to truces. We continued to build works, just as we did at any other time. We totally ignored such things. We were not

RAILWAY STATION ON THE ROAD FROM EL CANEY TO SANTIAGO.
(Used by Americans as hospital and guardhouse.)

more than five hundred yards — four hundred or five hundred yards — from the earthworks the Spanish occupied. They stood there on their works and looked at us, apparently in amazement."

The boys were there to take Santiago; and they did not propose to be caught unprepared by any Spanish fooling.

On that same twelfth of July came the commander-in-chief of the American army, General Nelson A. Miles, not to interfere in the campaign, but to be on hand at its close, even waiving his own suggestions in deference to Shafter's firm assurance that the enemy were "going to surrender."

Surrender they did at last. Bluff and diplomacy both gave in. At nine o'clock on the morning of Thursday, the fourteenth of July, the white flag came fluttering out from the Spanish lines. Then, in the shelter of the usual ceiba tree, General Shafter, the American, met General Toral, the Spaniard; a commission was appointed to draw up terms of capitulation; under the same ceiba tree the commissioners met, and, sitting on the ground, with a board on a camp stool for a table, they drew up and wrote out in Spanish and in English the terms of the surrender.

At five o'clock on the afternoon of July 16, the capitulation was signed. The news spread quickly. It climbed the hill to the trenches; it ran around the hills to the rifle-pits; it rushed to the front; it travelled to the rear, until the whole army, from El Caney to Aguadores and from San Juan to Siboney, had heard the welcome news.

Up to the boys in the trenches a horseman came spurring; he galloped along the line, and the soldiers knew, as they clambered out of the rifle-pits, that he bore good news for them.

He waved his hand in assurance and emphasis.

"What is it?" "What you got?" came the excited demands.

"Boys," shouted the messenger, quite as excitedly, "don't you cheer! We don't want to make those Dagoes feel too bad. But say, General Toral has agreed to surrender. That's straight. I got it from headquarters. They surrender."

No cheering! That was the order, out of respect to the defeated foemen. But all along that line of trenches a thousand hats were tossed high in air, while men jumped up and down for joy, and, as one marked time, the noiseless cheer that no one but themselves could hear went whispering along the line in a hoarse but voiceless chorus and to measured time: —

"Rah! rah! rah! Tiger!!"

Then, in a broad field before the gates of Santiago, General Shafter with his general officers and their staffs and a guard of one hundred men met General Toral, the Spanish commander, with an equal following. Standing before his troops,

WHY THEY CHEERED IN THE TRENCHES 259

General Toral, with presented sword, said, "I surrender the Spanish troops under my command and this place."

The Spanish officers and troops presented arms.

"I accept the surrender in behalf of the government of the United States," replied General Shafter.

"NO CHEERING!"

(How the boys in the trenches received the news of Toral's surrender.)

Then the Spanish flag dropped from the governor's palace in the city; the American soldiers presented arms in salute, and two and two the American officers and their escort rode through the gate of Santiago. At the governor's palace all the civil officers of the town received them. Lunch was served, and then as the clock on the cathedral struck the hour of noon, while the plaza was filled with a watching throng, and before the open doors were grouped the American officers and their staffs with one hundred men picked from the cavalry and infantry, Lieutenant Miley of General Shafter's staff ran up the stars and stripes to the top of the flagpole on the governor's palace.

The officers stood with uncovered heads; the soldiers presented arms; the band of the Sixth Cavalry struck up the "Star-Spangled Banner," the artillery fired a salute of twenty-one guns, and as Old Glory streamed from the conquered staff, all the world knew that the city of Santiago with all its defences and a Spanish army of twenty-three thousand men with all its arms and munitions of war had surrendered to the victorious American general, who had been sent to do a quick job quickly, and had done it!

And once more all the boys in the trenches and in the camps cheered for the flag, the republic, the army, and themselves. The men of the gun-deck and the turret, the men of the trench and the battery, had fought their fight and won the day. Santiago had fallen; an army had surrendered, and the President telegraphed to the general: —

WHY THEY CHEERED IN THE TRENCHES

"The President of the United States sends to you and your brave army the profound thanks of the American people for the brilliant achievements at Santiago, resulting in the surrender of the city and all of the Spanish troops and territory under General Toral.

"Your splendid command has endured not only the hardships and sacrifices incident to campaign and battle, but in stress of heat and weather has triumphed over obstacles which would have overcome men less brave and determined. One and all have displayed the most conspicuous gallantry, and earned the gratitude of the nation. The hearts of the people turn with tender sympathy to the sick and wounded. May the Father of Mercies protect and comfort them."

At noon on July 17 the thanks of the President were read to every regiment in the army before Santiago.

And once again the boys along ten miles of trenches and in the camp of the reserves cheered in approval and cried, "Hurrah for us!"

CHAPTER XIV

HOW THE FLAG FLOATED OVER PORTO RICO

GENERAL MILES.

ALTHOUGH General Miles, the commander-in-chief of the army, came down to Santiago, just before the surrender, as I have told you, to see how things were getting on, he did not stay there long.

In spite of some discomforts, some "shortages" as to food and supplies, and some heedlessness as to sanitary and health regulations in a hot, wet, Cuban season, General Miles found few things to criticise and less to change. He realized, as did few of the people who criticised unwittingly, that a short and sharp campaign in the heat of a tropical summer means much risk; but it was a campaign, in this case, that was imperative.

"Go with your force to capture garrison at Santiago and assist in capturing harbor and fleet," the "rush orders" to General Shafter had read. So, slighting many things that were important but not absolutely necessary for a short and sharp campaign, General Shafter rushed in to make quick work of it.

He did make quick work of it — and thorough, too. As the commissioners appointed by the President to make a full and unhampered investigation of the conduct of the war said in their report of February 12, 1899: —

"Owing to the lack of necessary transports, the means of land transportation during the Santiago campaign was painfully deficient, but, in spite of the absence of this almost absolutely necessary portion of the equipment of a well-trained command, the army drove the enemy before it, captured their outposts, pushed them behind their main defences, drove their fleet from Santiago bay to absolute destruction as it faced the navy of our country, and, finally, after most gallant fighting under a tropical sun, amid most adverse conditions, captured a strongly fortified city and received as prisoners of war over twenty-three thousand Spanish soldiers.

This was a grand record, in spite of adverse conditions — it was grand, even because of them. But General Miles, a brave soldier, an Indian fighter of long and triumphant experience, and a man who knew how to profit by the experiences

A BULLOCK CART IN PORTO RICO.
(A familiar sight in West Indian towns.)

of others, determined that, in the work he had to do, these "adverse conditions" should not exist, or, at least, should be reckoned for and discounted in advance.

The "work" he had to do was the occupation and subjugation of the Island of Porto Rico,

Spain's last possession in her former American Empire.

You will remember that the first plan of the War Department, before the invasion of Cuba, had been to possess itself of Porto Rico and use the island as a base of supplies and of operation against the Spaniards in Cuba. But Cervera's fleet and the Santiago campaign had changed all that; and the war had begun in Cuba.

None the less, though, was the wisdom of occupying Porto Rico felt at the War Department, and, as soon as the worst of the Santiago campaign seemed over, General Miles, who was to conduct in person the invasion of the smaller island, made ready for his Porto Rican campaign.

Long in advance of this, the island had been carefully and secretly studied by Captain Whitney, of the Engineers, who, says Mr. Davis, "at the greatest personal risk a man can run, had, two months before the army reached it, carefully studied out the entire island, its roads and harbors, so that not only the army, but the navy also relied upon and used his drawings and notes." There are other things besides marching and fighting, you see, that are necessary to success in war. How little we think of the silent, secret work done beforehand; how little of the humane, healing work done afterward. A campaign is not all battle; courage is not merely shooting, charging, and planting the flag. The Secret Service and the Red Cross Society have also their roll of heroes.

Still, battle is conflict, and it was necessary for General Miles to prepare beforehand for all the shooting and charging and planting the flag that might devolve upon his army of invasion. So he had everything fully gone over and mapped out in advance. Sailing for Santiago, ostensibly with reënforcements for Shafter's army, his troops were really intended for the campaign in Porto Rico, in case Santiago could get along without them.

After a few days before Santiago, he decided that the campaign so nearly closed there could be finished without the help of his men, and on the afternoon of Thursday, the twenty-first of July, he set sail from Guantanamo with an army of thirty-five hundred men, on eight transports, convoyed by a battleship, a cruiser, and six small war-vessels, some of which, like the plucky yacht *Gloucester*, had done splendid service with Sampson's fleet.

If you look at your map of Porto Rico, you will notice that, as it rises from the sea five

HOW THE FLAG FLOATED OVER PORTO RICO 267

hundred miles and more to the east of Cuba, with Haiti lying between, it looks like a big rectangular block, as indeed it is; for we are told that it has so few irregularities in its outline

THE CASA BLANCA.

(Or White House, the ancient castle of Ponce de Leon, the *Conquistadore*, in San Juan, Porto Rico.)

that its surface covers more than eighty-eight per cent of a real mathematical rectangle.

The island of Porto Rico is one hundred and eight miles long and thirty-seven miles wide. It is cut nearly through the middle by a range of mountains, running from east to west, and it is seamed with rivers and streams, some of them of fair size and depth. It has a population of eight hundred thousand, — San Juan, its capital, on the north coast, having twenty-four thousand inhabitants, and Ponce, on the south coast, having thirty-eight thousand.

General Miles's plan of invasion was to capture Ponce, on the south coast, and from there as a base to send four parallel columns of troops across the island, — one at the east end, one at the west, and two between, — who as they marched should drive all the Spaniards before them, the columns gradually heading toward San Juan on the north coast, where the enemy, being thus all carefully "rounded up," would be "corralled" and finally captured in the capital. It was as neat and clean and thorough a plan of campaign as ever this veteran Indian fighter had conceived and executed; and he had "rounded up" the Sioux after Custer's defeat and "corralled" the Nez Perces at Cow Island.

Since Columbus discovered the island in 1493, and Ponce de Leon settled it in 1510, Porto Rico had withstood and defeated four English invasions, Spain had crushed out two island insurrections, and the flag of Spain still floated as the *conquistadores* had planted it in possession

HOW THE FLAG FLOATED OVER PORTO RICO

and authority. Now, like a blast from the north, came the sons of the English and other men of vigorous stock to drive out the men who for four hundred years had ruled as masters of this beautiful summer isle.

But now the Spanish masters of Porto Rico had no fleet to protect them, no army to reënforce them, no help to depend upon but their own valor and persistence. The Porto Ricans, themselves, after four hundred years of Spanish rule, were willing and even anxious to exchange it for American possession; and, save for that debatable and uncertain factor of Spanish honor which has played so important and fluctuating a part in the romance and achievements of Spain from the Cid to Don Quixote and from Numantia to Saragossa, the Spanish army in Porto Rico might better have surrendered at once to the American invaders.

The American invaders coasted along the northern shore of Haiti and Santo Domingo, and every one in the fleet, excepting the general in command, decided that they were heading straight for San Juan, which, you remember, Admiral Sampson visited and bombarded while on a hunt for Cervera's elusive fleet. But, when off the Mona passage which divides Porto Rico from Santo Domingo, General Miles directed the fleet to turn south into the wide passage and announced to his officers that he was bound for Ponce on the southern coast.

Fifteen miles west of the city of Ponce is the little port of Guanica. The American expedition appeared off the town at daylight, on July 25. At once, Wainwright, in the yacht *Gloucester*, steamed into the harbor, silenced the surprised Spanish blockhouse defenders, and then, landing a force of blue-jackets, hauled down the Spanish flag, ran up the stars and stripes, and "wig-wagged" to the fleet that Guanica was won! Then the troops disembarked from the transports, the frightened Guanicans came streaming back from the hills in welcome, and the American landing on the soil of Porto Rico had been accomplished without an injury.

Ponce, as I have told you, was to be the basis of operations in the Porto Rican campaign, and Ponce, therefore, must be captured at once. For this purpose an advance was sent against the little village of Yauco, where the railroad to Ponce begins, and companies of the Sixth Massachusetts and of the Sixth Illinois volunteers, com-

A PORTO RICAN GARDEN.

ing upon the enemy intrenched on a hill near the village of Yauco, at once engaged them in a skirmish and charge, defeating and driving them back.

Meantime the battleship *Massachusetts* with four of the smaller war-vessels had steamed down to Ponce to blockade the harbor and combine with the army for its capture. But while the combination was forming, a bright young sailor-lad, Ensign Curtin of the *Dixie*, was sent on shore by his commander. He bore a letter demanding the surrender of the port and city of Ponce; and he was so determined-looking a boy and had so evidently the air of the "conquering hero," that the captain of the port was visibly impressed by this combination of sailor-boy and battleships.

Now the city of Ponce lies four miles inland from the port of Ponce; but the captain of the port felt confident that his superior officer, the commandant of Ponce, would deem it wise to surrender the city if the valiant young American officer would honor him with a visit and ride up to the city with his letter.

The idea of an ensign of the American navy riding off to confer with a Spanish commander for the surrender of a city of forty thousand inhabitants was not to be thought of! It was clearly the Spanish commander's duty to come to the port and surrender to the ensign. So he demanded at once that the commandant at Ponce be "called up" on the telephone and informed that unless the port and city of Ponce were surrendered to the American forces within thirty minutes the warships would bombard immediately. The telephone tinkled and buzzed, and the ensign's message went over the 'phone to Ponce.

What could the commandant do? He yielded at once to the stern demand of the determined young ensign, and thus, for the first time in history, a city was summoned and surrendered by telephone; and the nation will not forget the name and triumphal bearing of Ensign Curtin of the *Dixie*.

Next day, the twenty-ninth of July, the port and town were actually occupied by the troops, and the chief city of Porto Rico came into the possession of the invaders without a blow.

It was but the beginning of the same experience all over the island. For so complete and effective was General Miles's plan of campaign, so ready were the people of Porto Rico to change flags and, from Spanish subjects become possible American citizens, that the army of invasion was greeted, says Mr. Church, "not as conquerors, but as deliverers," and instead of a bombardment General Miles met them with proclamations and promises, and his men had to defend themselves from embraces rather than ambuscades.

The friendliness of the people and the way in which they helped rather than hindered the American occupation furnished the key, so Mr. Church declares, "to the bold and rapid advance ordered by General Miles in all directions."

His advance was, indeed, bold and rapid. Three

ports on the southern coast — Ponce, Guanica, and Arrayo — were occupied, and at once the little army, now reënforced by new arrivals to nearly eleven thousand men, commenced its march by four well-considered routes around and across the

A MOUNTAIN BATTERY.
(Ready to start for the advance across Porto Rico.)

island, with the capital city of San Juan, on the north coast, as the objective point.

The divisions marched promptly and triumphantly. Town after town surrendered, and American flags of occupation were in such demand that temporary ones had to be painted by soldier decorators and permanent ones telegraphed for to Washington. At various points the Spanish troops resisted the American advance — at Hermiqueras and Rio Comas, at Aibonito and Guayama and other minor points; but these were all little else than skirmishes, the one at Hermiqueras being the most important, and all of them being won by the Americans at an insignificant loss in killed and wounded.

It was on the twelfth of August that the artillery of General Wilson's division of General Brooke's command had advanced their guns to the pass of Aibonito, near the town of Guayama, from which the fine military road runs straight to San Juan.

The Spaniards intrenched upon the hills were called upon to surrender, but the colonel commanding them sent back the plucky answer: "Tell General Wilson if he wishes to avoid the further shedding of blood to stay where he is."

But General Wilson did not intend to stay where he was. He was determined to reduce and occupy the Spanish intrenchments on the hills; so he advanced his position, planted his artillery, and prepared to give the Spanish colonel defiance for defiance.

Further along General Wilson's line, where General Brooke was watching his forward movement, Battery B of the Pennsylvania artillery had pushed on its guns to command the Spanish position to the left of Guayama. The piece was trained, the shell was in its chamber, range and sight were both arranged, and the gunner had just sprung backward for the discharge, when down the hard road came the sound of clattering hoofs, and a lieutenant of the Signal Corps galloped on the scene. In one hand he waved a despatch, with the other he pulled in his panting horse, while all the time he shouted the command:

"Peace, peace! Cease firing! Peace has been declared!"

The gunner dropped his string; the gun stood silent; the men of the battery gave a groan of displeasure.

"Why couldn't he have waited just a minute?" they demanded, as the lieutenant flung himself from the saddle and handed his despatches to General Brooke. "We'd have given those Dagoes just one last thing to remember us by."

The lieutenant was right. Peace had been declared; or, at least, the Spanish government had proposed an armistice, and through the French minister at Washington had signed the preliminary agreement for peace. At once all hostile

"CEASE FIRING! PEACE HAS BEEN DECLARED!"

operations on land and sea were stopped, and the flag which had come in armed invasion to Porto Rico, stayed wherever it was raised. The union of forces for the occupation of San Juan was peaceably made, and all the elaborate plans for the military conquest of the island yielded to the demands of peace.

But the island so happily invaded at such little loss, thanks to the careful plans of the commanding general and the spontaneous uprising of the people, had passed into the possession of the United States to stay. The permanent annexation of the island was declared to be the determination of the United States; the decision was joyfully accepted by the people of that land of summer, and, after four hundred years of wasteful occupation and stupid misrule, the Spanish banner fell from its staff and the flag of the Union floated over Porto Rico.

CHAPTER XV

WHY GENERAL MERRITT PLAYED JACKSON AT MANILA

ON the very day when that lieutenant of the signal corps galloped along the lines in Porto Rico shouting "peace!" to the expressed dissatisfaction of the gunners of Battery B, it was raining heavily in far-off Manila.

There was nothing strange about that, for it was the rainy season at Manila, and the camp of the Americans on Manila Bay was wet and soggy from three weeks of perpetual rain. But the boys in the camp did not find so much fault with the rain as they did over the delay. There they were, soldier boys from America, spoiling for a fight; there, in and about the old walled city, was the enemy; and the Spanish flag still floated above the ramparts and walls of Manila!

"Why don't we go in and chase 'em out?" was their frequent grumbling query. "That's what we came here for, wasn't it?"

Since we stopped that July day with the

advance of the relief expedition and so surprised the governor of Guam, a small army of United States troops had sailed into Manila harbor. They counted ten thousand men in all, regulars and volunteers, in three divisions, with Major-General Wesley Merritt in command, while two more warships, the *Monadnock* and the *Monterey*, reënforced Admiral Dewey's fleet.

The Western boys who made up the bulk of the invading army — volunteers in regiments from Oregon, Nebraska and Idaho, Minnesota, Washington, and both the Dakotas, Colorado, Wyoming and Nevada, California, Utah and Kansas, with some from Pennsylvania also, and a few regiments of regulars — were impatient to get at the Spaniards at once, not appreciating the fact that, in war, diplomacy plays almost as important a part as fighting.

Admiral Dewey and General Merritt had a number of things to "arrange." The insurgent Filipinos, strengthened in their endeavor for independence by the American declaration of war and Dewey's remarkable victory, gathered in force before Manila, proclaimed the Philippine republic, declared Emilio Aguinaldo generalissimo and president of the revolutionary government, captured over sixteen thousand Spanish prisoners, and demanded recognition and alliance from the United States.

But neither Admiral Dewey nor General Merritt was authorized to treat with the so-called Philippine republic, nor to recognize Aguinaldo as its president. Their duty was to capture or expel the Spaniards from the Philippines and assert the temporary authority of the United States as occupiers and possessors of conquered Spanish territory; in no way would they recognize or countenance, officially, the claims or desires of the insurgent Filipinos, whose army, thirty thousand strong, had gathered about beleaguered Manila.

This was no easy work in those peculiar surroundings, where much of the comfort of the army depended upon the relations with the natives; neither was it easy to hold in check the unfriendliness of the German and the French naval officers, who openly displayed their sympathy for Spain, and who, again and again, as I have told you in a former chapter, pushed the forbearance of Admiral Dewey almost to the breaking point.

More than this, the main object of the expedition — the conquest of the Spanish forces in the

Philippines — claimed their first thought; but even in this operation other things than "just fighting" needed to be considered. Ammunition and supplies for the troops must be landed and distributed; the non-combatants and foreign citizens in Manila must be given time for removal, and due notice of bombardment and attack must be communicated, in the interests of humanity.

On the twenty-fifth of July General Merritt had arrived with the last detachment of troops; an intrenched camp had been made in a rice field near the shore of the bay, between Cavite and Manila, to which had been given the name of Camp Dewey, and the outposts had been advanced to within two miles and a half of the Spanish works.

On the night of July 31, the Spanish soldiers made an attack on the American intrenchments, in the midst of a fierce midnight storm, but our boys were ready for them, and the attack was repulsed as, with a rousing cheer, the California troops charged through the rain to the support of the Pennsylvania boys, and silenced the Spanish fire. Ten men were killed and thirty wounded in that fight before the Spanish outworks; but it showed the temper and proved the valor of the American troops, and, save by a few feints at attack and a harmless artillery fire to which our boys were ordered to pay no attention, their efforts to provoke the Americans to a fight ceased, and our land and naval force prepared for the final attack.

This came on the thirteenth of August. On the seventh, Admiral Dewey and General Merritt, having summoned the Spanish commander to surrender, gave him forty-eight hours to remove the women and children; after which, unless the city surrendered, the bombardment and assault of Manila would begin.

As there was really no place to which the helpless non-combatants could be sent, the city being entirely invested by the American troops on one side and the rebel Filipinos on the other, the admiral and the general, when the forty-eight hours had expired, sent another summons to the Spaniard, showing him his absolute helplessness and hopelessness in case a joint attack was made; and again they formally demanded his surrender.

Like all Spanish commanders, the general at Manila shirked his responsibilities, and said he must refer the matter to the home authorities at Madrid, and was therefore powerless in the matter. Whereupon the American commanders, seeing that a fight was the only way to settle the

THE APPROACH TO MANILA.
(The old bridge over the Pasig.)

question, called a council of war on the eleventh of August, and explained to the generals of divisions the plans for the joint attack.

Next day — that same twelfth of August on which the galloping messengers of peace roused the trenches before Santiago and stopped the battle in Porto Rico, the troops before Manila, ignorant of what was happening ten thousand miles away, were gathering in the pouring rain for the storming of Manila.

At four o'clock on the morning of Saturday, the thirteenth, the camp was on the move, and the men began their march to the front. Out of the soggy camp, and along the muddy road, knee-deep in water, while the rain fell heavily, the Americans advanced, careless of the weather and the water so long as the forward movement meant business and the boys were to have a chance at the enemy.

Out in the bay the ships of the squadron were also in motion; and, as they started, the rain stopped, and the sky cleared, much to the relief of the jackies as well as the soldier boys; for if they were to see the fight, they said, they wanted regular " Dewey weather " — that glorious May-day over again.

The lead-colored fighting ships were stripped for action; awnings were ready to be thrown off, fires under the boilers needed only a stir to set them roaring, and every man in the fleet watched to see the signal "Close in" stream out from the yards of the *Olympia*.

The signal flew at last, and at nine o'clock on the morning of the thirteenth, while the land force was marching out of Camp Dewey on the beach, the fleet of Admiral Dewey, in assigned order, fell into line, and, with battle flags at mast and gaff, stood across the bay for Manila.

The fleets of neutral nations had been ordered from the zone of danger. Far down the bay, toward Corregidor, lay the German and Spanish warships, eight keels in all; but, close against the American right, the three warships of England ranged themselves — a warning, a protest, a barrier, if occasion arose, against any hostile movement on the part of the French or German fleet. England had decided against Spain, against all Europe, if need be, and ranged her fleet side by side with that of her "kin beyond sea," as Gladstone called the Americans.

And as Dewey's battle line swept across the bay toward Manila on that famous Saturday

GENERAL MERRITT AT MANILA 289

morning, the British flagship *Immortalité* steamed from her berth with her men manning the rigging, her officers drawn up at salute, her splendid band stationed on the quarterdeck. Right alongside the American flagship she steamed, and as she passed the *Olympia*, her band struck up, "The Star-Spangled Banner." Then her men and officers cheered in salute, and as the *Olympia* signalled the fleet to "break out the battle flags," and the Stars and Stripes streamed from every masthead, again the British band played — "See! the Conquering Hero Comes!" again the British sailors cheered in salute and God-speed, and with the friendly echoes still ringing in their ears the Yankee jackies sailed on to their last battle with Spain in the war of '98.

You remember, do you not, that when General Andrew Jackson fought his famous battle of the cotton bales before New Orleans, on the eighth of January, in the year 1815, peace had already been declared between England and America. But of this "Old Hickory" knew nothing, for there were no telegraphs then, mails were slow and long in coming, and New Orleans was really farther from Washington than is Manila in this day of quick connections.

Telegraphs and mails were better in the day of Merritt and Dewey. But Hong Kong was the nearest telegraphic point to Manila, and it took three days for a despatch boat to steam across the China Sea with telegrams. So, when the thirteenth of August dawned, although hostilities were ordered to cease and peace had been arranged, the soldiers and sailors at far-off Manila had no knowledge of it, and General Merritt, all unwittingly, was about to play in the Philippines the part of General Andrew Jackson.

The navy opened the ball. Moving in line of battle, the *Olympia* leading, the warships steamed up the bay, and at 9.45 o'clock a shot from the *Olympia's* forward turret went flying over the water.

Well in front of the walled city of Manila lay the old Malate fort, the chief artillery defence of the town. A line of trenches connected this fort with a blockhouse and covered the main approach to Manila along the Calle Real, or Royal Road.

Admiral Dewey had no desire to bombard the city itself, filled with helpless non-combatants. He therefore ordered that the warships should not do this unless the batteries to the north of the Malate fort opened fire on the fleet. So the rest of the squadron floated silent while the *Olympia*, the *Raleigh*, and the little *Petrel* plumped their shot against the old Malate fort and against the connecting intrenchments.

A STREET IN MANILA.
(Showing signs of war's destruction.)

Meantime, General Greene, Merritt's second in command, had ordered his artillery to support the fire of the ships, and soon the field-guns were sweeping the ramp of the old fort. Then, as the troops drew nearer the Spanish line, General Greene ordered a charge, and up to the line and over the intrenchments went two companies of

Colorado boys, the second battalion, an instant after, springing to their support.

Before the vigorous rush of the Westerners the Spaniards refused to stand. They fled from their trenches to the cover of the fort; but nothing stopped their pursuers. Over the intrenchments went one column; up the beach and through the bamboo trail charged another. They forded the creek; they rushed the breastwork; they forced the entrance to the old fort, which for centuries had withstood attack.

But not a Spaniard was there to greet them. Dismayed by the fire of the fleet and the resistless rush of the troops, the garrison had deserted the fort, and, flying for the nearest refuge, had sheltered themselves behind the breastworks and within the blockhouse in the rear of the Malate, from which point of vantage they opened a worrying fire upon the captors of the fort.

But the captors of the fort thought more of glory than of danger from Spanish riflemen, and when Lieutenant-colonel McCoy, of the First Colorado, climbed the flagpole and tore down the Spanish colors that streamed over the fort, and in their place ran up the Stars and Stripes, then such a cheer rang out from ship and shore, from navy and army alike, that the Spaniards "shook in their shoes," and concluded there was no resisting " these terrible *Americanos*."

While this was going on, other columns of Colorado troops had cleared the trenches connecting the fort and the blockhouse, and crossing the bridge that spanned the creek, pushed boldly along the Royal Road. Far off at the northeast the Spanish fire was directed toward them, but with so little effect that, when their comrades came to their support, the regimental band stationed itself in the captured trenches and began to play an inspiriting march. Then up from the beach and over the conquered earthworks came the reserves, as if on parade, marching in column with all flags flying. And when the colors trooped within the Spanish lines, the boys all cheered again.

As this movement on the left ended in triumph, the regulars and artillery on the right advanced against the trenches and the blockhouse, and, in the face of a hot fire from the trenches, swept the line, drove the Spaniards into the shelter of the blockhouse, and pushed their way into the outskirts of the city.

Just outside the green, moss-grown walls of old Manila, on the southern side of the town, stretches the beautiful promenade known as the Lunetta — the fashionable resort of Manila in times of peace, the pleasure ground upon which many a file of rebel Filipinos has been lined up and shot by Spanish soldiers for wishing to be free.

As the advancing column of Americans came up the Royal Road to where it crosses the Lunetta and filed into that splendid parade, the soldier boys cheered again. For there, ahead of them, was fluttering about the western bastion of the city walls the white flag of surrender. Word was passed rapidly to the rear, General Greene came galloping up, the rear of the column was ordered to double quick, and soon, beneath the gray walls of the old Spanish capital, moat-encircled and flanked by outer defences such as never these modern American boys had seen, massed before the main sallyport or gateway to the fortified town, with colors flying in the strong sea-breeze and expectancy waiting with it all, one-half the American army of invasion waited while, within the walls, General Merritt decided the fate of the Philippines.

Decision came speedily. "Yielding to superior force," the Spanish captain-general surrendered the city and fortifications of Manila with all the Spanish troops therein. Eleven thousand Spanish soldiers capitulated as prisoners of war; the American troops marched in through the old, old gateway to occupy the town; sentries were posted at every gate to protect the city from the over-confident and spoil-demanding insurgent Filipinos. Above the governor-general's palace streamed Old Glory in token of possession, while below in the garden of the palace, captured munitions of war were piled high in picturesque disarray.

Manila was won. After four hundred years of Spanish misrule, the wonderfully promising Pacific island-group of which it was the capital passed into the possession of the vigorous republic of the New World. Dewey with his fleet, and Merritt with his soldier boys, had forced down the flag which, in all those four hundred years of Spanish occupation, had never yet been lowered, save when the English stormed and held the city for ransom in 1762; and, the very day after peace had been declared, General Wesley Merritt, like Jackson at New Orleans, had fought a needless but spirited fight, and won an unnecessary but glorious victory.

CHAPTER XVI

THE THINGS THAT HELPED

THUS, steadily, from victory to victory, from conquest to conquest, the war went forward, until all men saw that the end was in sight, and all men knew what that end would be. Of every victory and of every conquest the soldiers and sailors of the United States were the direct instruments; but as instruments are of little value save as they are used by skilled hands, so in war the skill in handling rests first upon the brain that guides the instrument, and next upon the outside helps that keep the instrument keen and sharp.

By this, of course, you know, I mean that the army and navy of the United States won swift success in our war with Spain because of their own valor, the way in which that valor was rightly directed and guided by "the men at the head," and also by the things that helped.

There is little doubt that General Miles's assertion was true that fifty thousand volunteers would be a sufficient number to summon to battle, provided the regular army was proportionately increased. For, as you have seen, the short and sharp campaign against Santiago demanded the actual services of less than twenty thousand men; and the operations in far-off Manila did not at first require over twelve thousand fighting men. The actual forces of the regular army would have sufficed, so far as real fighting in the field was concerned; while a smaller and better-concentrated force would have obviated the crowding or "congesting," as it is called, of men in camp and in transport.

But in our war with Spain, the moral effect played quite as important a part as the actual operations, and the call for two hundred thousand volunteers, so quickly and surprisingly obeyed, was a revelation to Spain and to the rest of the world of the spirit of patriotism that dominated America, and showed that "business-loving" America when once aroused was not to be trifled with.

We know that volunteers far in excess of the required number were quick to answer the call of the President, but it is also a fact that, even before his call, days and weeks even before war was declared, application for service had come to the War Department in such numbers that they could not even be acknowledged, much less acted upon. A week before war was declared to exist, these applications for appointment in the service amounted to nearly eighteen thousand, while at the same time offers of service exceeded a million of men.

"CAPRON'S PET."
(One of the "helps" trained on Santiago.)

Was not that the best sort of an answer to those halting and unpatriotic doubters who declared that a war with Spain over Cuba would never be popular, and that no one would volunteer for such a war? So, you see, the first of "the things that helped" was the American people themselves. They helped, too, in that wonderful and spontaneous subscription to the big war loan, of which I told you — the authorized loan by the people to the government of two hundred millions of dollars which, limited to small amounts, was subscribed for by the people many times over — five to one, at least. And money, cheerfully loaned by a people to prosecute a people's war, helps wonderfully.

Then the people themselves helped, individually; how much they helped we shall never really know. I do not mean the officials, the department workers, or the soldiers and sailors. I mean the people themselves. There were people of means and position, like Miss Helen Gould, who gave so freely and so gracefully of her money, her time, and her ability as to shame those of equal means who showed no sign of practical patriotism, while Congress officially thanked her for her patriotic interest, and the nation honored and esteemed her; there were people of no means and of unrecognized position who, from the children in the schools to the quiet worker in the country village, sacrificed what was much to them to strengthen, cheer, or help the soldiers in the field. The lessons of the Civil War, that time of superhuman sacrifice, in the North and South alike, had not been in vain, and the patriotism of 1861 bore its fruit in the patriotism of 1898.

How widespread was that patriotism the response of the people in every section of the land amply showed. There were critics and fault-finders, as there always are and always will be when great deeds are afoot, but what the republic started out to do, it did! and criticism and fault-finding proved but blunted and blundering shafts. From every section came the patriots and heroes. Party lines were wiped away, sectional lines were obliterated, state and local rivalries were forgotten, and young and old, ready to uphold the national government, seemed possessed of that spirit that lived in one of Webster's grandest speeches, "I — I, too, am an American."

When Hobson of the Navy, welcomed by the cheers of an army, came out from his Santiago prison to liberty, he was greeted by General Joseph Wheeler, commanding the cavalry division of Shafter's army. With the general was his son, a lieutenant on his father's staff, while another son was on the *Columbia* of the blockading squadron, and his daughter was nursing the sick and wounded at Siboney. "It was," says Mr. Hobson, "a remarkable picture of devotion, one of the most remarkable in history. This general, who with so much gallantry had led Confederate cavalry, was now in the front rank of the Union forces, and with him almost his entire family, all in trying positions and braving the worst hardships. I had felt all the time," he adds, "that there was in the Southern heart nothing but the truest loyalty; the occasion for proof had at last come, the fulfilment of a long-felt desire, and henceforth the fact must be recognized by all parts of the country."

"The state of Florida," wrote Mr. Davis from the camp of the Second Massachusetts under the pines of Lakeland, near Tampa, "is not very far from the Commonwealth of Massachusetts when a boy is dying under a tent, and a woman stands outside the little chapel crying because the officers had not allowed her to take the sick soldier to her own house. She was only one of many women each of whom came to the camp to ask if she could not nurse the soldier, or bring him home with her, so that she might feel that she was doing something for the cause; so that his mother up in Massachusetts might feel that some other mother had been with him at the last." In the union of feeling and sympathy which brought all the sections of the great republic into one helpful, undivided family the war with Spain was worth all it cost in blood and treasure, and in this mighty and spontaneous work all the people helped.

And when, later, not one but hundreds of soldiers lay sick and suffering from wounds or fever, when food was scarce, and in the pest-ridden towns or in the crowded huts beyond the camps the starving reconcentrados and refugees of Cuba begged for bread, one other humane element of modern warfare did a noble work, knowing neither friend nor foe, knowing only the dictates of Christ's humanity, under the old crusading sign of the Red Cross.

A NOBLE HELPER.
(The Red Cross "soup line" in Santiago.)

From the very beginning of the war, from the gathering at Tampa to the last days, after surrender and even after peace, the American National Red Cross was in the field to succor the suffering Americans, Spanish, and Cubans. Upon its great black steamer, the *State of Texas*, "flying from her mainmast head the white flag emblazoned with the red Greek cross of the Geneva Convention," were the headquarters of Miss Clara Barton and her staff of trained surgeons, nurses, and field officers; and from Port Tampa to Santiago, in all the days of war and sickness, the American National Red Cross proved itself one of the things that helped mightily.

"Working in conjunction with the government authorities," said President McKinley, "and under their sanction and approval, and with the enthusiastic coöperation of many patriotic women and societies in the various states, the Red Cross has fully maintained its already high reputation for intense earnestness and ability to exercise the noble purposes of its international organization, thus justifying the confidence and support which it has received at the hands of American people. To the members and officers of this society and all who aided them in philanthropic work, the sincere and lasting gratitude of the soldiers and the public is due, and is freely accorded. In tracing these events we are constantly reminded of our obligations to the Divine Master for His watchful care over us and His safe guidance, for which the nation makes reverent acknowledgment, and offers humble prayer for the continuance of His favor."

It was said, indeed, by certain critics of our military and naval movements that we owed most of our success to the watchful care and safe guidance of this ever watchful Providence; that we had nothing but luck and good fortune from the start; that when our transports or roving boats should naturally have been sunk or blown up or wrecked, they sailed on to success over summer seas; that, in fact, as one of the generals on the invading fleet declared, "This is God Almighty's war, and we are only His agents."

But while good fortune doubtless did attend the voyage of the invading army and the movements of our fleets, it was also largely a proof of the saying that "the Lord helps those who help themselves." For though much may have been omitted, much was also done; and among the many things that helped was the wisdom of the Navy Department in adding to the sea-power of the republic among the steam vessels purchased, hired, or given to the government, the four "ocean greyhounds" of the American Line, officially known as the "International Navigation Company." These swift and beautiful boats, known to thousands of ocean travellers as the *St. Paul*, *St. Louis*, *New York*, and *Paris*, were fitted up as swift scout boats or auxiliary cruisers, the last two being rechristened the *Yale* and *Harvard*, in honor of two leading American universities. They did splendid service, in connection with the blockading fleet and under rush orders from the admiral, while more than once their batteries came in play for the bombardment of Spanish fortifications or the spirited attacks upon Spanish warships.

One such spirited attack has become historic,— the plucky fight between the *St. Paul* and the

THE ST. PAUL AND THE TERROR.
(Off San Juan, June 22.)

Terror, on the twenty-second of June, off the Porto Rican port of San Juan.

The *St. Paul* was supplied with a battery of twelve guns — five-inch, six-pounders, three-pounders, and Hotchkiss. She was commanded by the brave Captain Sigsbee of the slaughtered *Maine;* and when on that June day a Spanish cruiser and a torpedo-boat destroyer sailed out from San Juan to sink the *St. Paul*, the ocean greyhound was ready for them.

The cruiser was soon out of the race; but the destroyer, *Terror*, stuck to her work determinedly, for the *St. Paul* was an attractive target, and the *Terror*, with her swift movements, six guns, torpedo outfit, and tremendous speed, was a formidable adversary. There was a good deal of darting and dodging and firing, but to no advantage on either side, until at last the big liner got the true range and sent a straight shot at the *Terror*, raking her fore and aft. Wounded by this shot, the *Terror* checked her desperate dash, and turned for safety; but as she did so, her broadside was exposed, and a keen-eyed gunner on the *St. Paul*, seeing his chance, let fly a five-inch shot, so correctly aimed that it tore its way into the *Terror's* engine-room, disabling her completely, and puncturing her hull so badly that if the Spanish cruiser had not grappled and towed her inshore she would have sunk at once in wreck.

"I will sink the *St. Paul* or be sunk in the attempt," said the captain of the *Terror*, as he rushed to destroy the American.

"Well, sir," commented one of the *St. Paul's* men, "that Dago skipper came pretty near getting one of the things he was looking for." What with Sigsbee striking at the *Terror*, and Wainwright destroying the *Pluton*, the former captain and executive officer of the ill-fated *Maine* took grim toll for damages from the ships of Spain. In both cases, memory was one of the things that helped.

But if memory helped, so, too, did sleepless, secret vigilance. None know how important in any war is the detective work performed by that department known as the Secret Service. Its agents work silently and all unknown; its heroes fall unnoticed and misunderstood; but upon its watchfulness and shrewdness much of the final victory depends.

It was so in the war with Spain. The agents of the Secret Service were everywhere; in Cuba, plotting with the insurgents; in Porto Rico, looking over the ground; in distant Hong Kong and Manila, studying the secrets of Spain; even in Spain itself, noting alike the political and military moves of the hostile nation; locating and sketching its defences; following the movements of Cervera's fleet before it sailed from Cadiz, and of Camara's fleet as it sailed through the Mediterranean to "slay" Dewey, only to be stopped and turned back useless at Suez.

You have seen how Lieutenant Rowan at the peril of his life penetrated the jungles, and crossing Spanish lines communicated with Garcia and his men; so, too, later in the war, did Lieutenant Victor Blue of the *Suwanee*, at the imminent peril of his life, land from the fleet blockading Santiago, penetrate to the insurgent camp, and with but three Cuban guides climb the hills within the Spanish lines, and actually see for himself and for the admiral that Cervera's fleet really did lie in the harbor of Santiago. Two weeks later he repeated this hazardous attempt, actually stealing his way within the intrenched Spanish lines, and again locating and noting the position of the cornered squadron.

In reporting the moves of the Spanish agents in Canada, in unmasking and undoing the French blockade-runner *Lafayette*, even after it had made the harbor of Havana, and in a thousand unheralded and unknown exploits of inestimable value to American success, did the perfectly organized Secret Service do valiant and helpful work.

Another valuable adjunct of the army and the navy in their work of war was the Signal Corps. Their work was difficult and dangerous. From " wig-wagging " the fleet from shore, or aiding the brave signalmen in the face of a killing Spanish fire at Guantanamo, to stretching telephone lines from camp to headquarters at Siboney and Sevila and to the front at Santiago, and navigating a war-balloon above the hostile lines, the duties of the Signal Corps were delicate, hazardous, and intricate.

"Its operations during the war," said the President in his report, "covered the electrical connection of all coast fortifications, the establishment of telephonic and telegraphic facilities for the camps at Manila, Santiago, and in Porto Rico. There were constructed three hundred miles of line at ten great camps, thus facilitating military movements from these points in a manner heretofore unknown in military administration. Field telegraph lines were established and maintained under the enemy's fire at Manila and later the Manila-Hong Kong cable was reopened. In Porto Rico cable communications were opened over a discontinued route, and on land the headquarters of the commanding officer were kept in telegraphic or telephonic communication with the division commanders on four different lines of operations. There was placed in Cuban waters a completely outfitted cable ship, with war cables and cable gear, suitable both for the destruction of communications belonging to the enemy and the establishment of our own. Two ocean cables were destroyed under the enemy's batteries at Santiago. The day previous to the landing of General Shafter's corps at Caimanera, within twenty miles of the landing place, cable

"TAKING HIS QUININE."
(How the hospital service helped.)

communications were established and a cable station opened, giving direct communication with the government at Washington. This service was invaluable to the executive in directing the operations of the army and navy. With a total force of over thirteen hundred the loss by disease in camp and field, officers and men included, was only five."

Brave fellows were those Signal Corps men. They were, so General Greely, the chief signal officer, declares, "the flower of the volunteer army." Their leaders were, he says, "highly trained officers in the prime of life, thoroughly skilled in the specialties of the corps, not only admirably fitted for administrative duties, but also capable of arduous campaigning. Not one of these officers was either invalided or obliged to quit his duties during the war, though they served at Santiago, in Porto Rico, and at Manila." As to the enlisted men, they could challenge, General Greely asserts, "any other corps or branch of the army to produce their equal for ability, intelligence, and amenability to discipline. Their service was uniformly marked by cheerfulness, zeal, and good conduct, and was characterized by that resourcefulness which is an especial characteristic of the typical American soldier."

Thanks to the Signal Corps, General Shafter at headquarters was in direct communication by telephone with his subordinate commanders, and these lines, General Greely reports, "were uninterruptedly maintained under the fire and during the progress of battle" up to within four hundred yards of the enemy and twenty-four hours in the day;

besides communicating with Admiral Sampson through a telephone stationed near Aguadores. General Shafter in twenty minutes could get a message to President McKinley or a reply from him, and in twenty seconds could communicate with his right, centre, and left. And at Manila, when the final assault came, so General Greely tells the nation, "one company of the Signal Corps ran the field telegraph line up to the open beach and established an advanced station under fire of the enemy's second line. Another party, led by Captain McKenna, marched up the beach with the firing line, their signal flags displayed so that the fire of the navy should fall in advance of the army, and, displaying these flags as the first emblems of the United States in the enemy's fort, established an advanced telegraph station under the fire of the enemy's second line and maintained communication with both wings of the army until the enemy's positions were carried."

Certainly, as brave as it is marvellous, is the method and equipment of the modern fighting man!

Other things helped. The mule, patient, maligned, ill-used, over-loaded, and unlovely beast of burden as he is, was in his humble way almost the salvation of the army at the front, when heavy military wagons could not travel the broken, watery roads, and the mule with his pack, passing ceaselessly in single file, was the only means of keeping up open and continuous communication with the distant base of supplies.

The teamster helped, sometimes almost heroically, as when "in the bloody San Juan" one held his team still under fire, because he had been told that the boys would need supplies or ammunition at the front, and he must be on hand to take them; and in the terrible night ride of the wounded to the hospitals at the rear, after the fight at San Juan, so Mr. Bonsall says, "I did not see a single instance of negligence or carelessness on the part of the teamsters and the hospital attendants who were in charge of the melancholy train." And this was in full range of the withering, unnerving Spanish fire in the gloom of the night.

The hospital service — that dreadful necessity in war — was also a mighty helper, — alas! too sadly needed for the sick in camp rather than for those hurt in war. At the front were field hospitals; there were the hospital ships, *Olivette* and *Solace* and *Bay State;* at the camps of concentration there were the usual camp hospitals; while at other points, in anticipation of possible need, general hospitals were established — at Key West, Florida; at Fort McPherson, Georgia; at Fort Thomas, Kentucky; at Chickamauga and Fortress Monroe and Fort Myer; while in order to transport the sick and wounded from the front to these hospitals what may be called the greater ambulance service was organized. "This consisted," says Dr. Dunham, "of several hospital ships, carefully and thoroughly equipped, fitted with medical supplies, and carrying surgeons and nurses, which were designed to ply between Cuba or Porto Rico and Key West, Tampa, or other coast cities. For distribution from Tampa a hospital train was provided, consisting of ten sleeping-cars and a dining-car, which made numerous trips between that port and various inland hospitals."

So, in many ways and through many departments of assistance and relief, of information, intelligence, and preparation, were there numberless things that helped on to success besides the valor of the soldier and the sailor. But they all served as contributors to the soldier's and sailor's success; for, as every one knows, the fighting man is in war the all-important personage; and while, in every branch of service, there are brave, self-sacrificing, heroic, and noble men and women, — from those who, at home or in the field, organize for assistance and relief, to those who sound the bugle, or cook the rations, or "stoke" the furnace, — after all, the interest and

SUPPLIES FOR THE CAMP.
(A snap-shot at Montauk.)

sympathy, and enthusiasm and applause, of the nation are given to those who are cared for and strengthened by the things that help — the soldier and sailor of the republic fighting in Cuba, or

Porto Rico, or far-distant Manila, that the word of the United States of America may be kept unbroken and humanity be established even at a fearful cost of life and treasure. For, in the grand result, humanity and progress will be the things that count, and in their service not a dollar nor a life will be found to have been spent in vain.

CHAPTER XVII

HOW THE WAR ENDED

WHEN the ships of Cervera's fleet went down in destruction on the Cuban coast and the Stars and Stripes streamed out in victory above the red-tiled roofs and yellow walls of captured Santiago, even Spain knew that the time had come to cry "Enough!" Spanish honor, which might have been saved by the evacuation and abandonment of Cuba, now confessed itself appeased only when, as a sacrifice to its excellent but uncertain demands, it had lost two fleets, two armies, and possession and sovereignty both in the Atlantic and the Pacific. We honor the brave, but we criticise the obstinate. One who reads Spanish history and Spanish romance can see how impossible it is for Don Quixote to play the part of the Cid Campeador.

On the very day that General Miles began his invasion of Porto Rico by the advance on Ponce, the twenty-sixth of July, 1898, the Spanish Minister of State at Madrid requested the French ambassador at Washington — there being no official representative of Spain in America — to ask the United States upon what terms peace could be arranged. The government of the United States at once made its reply, and on the seventh

SANTIAGO HARBOR AND THE MORRO.

(The wreck of the *Reina Mercedes* sunk by a shot from the fleet on July 6; this ship received Hobson as a prisoner from Cervera, and has now been raised and saved.)

of August Spain, through the French ambassador, accepted some of the demands of the United States unconditionally, but tried to modify others.

The United States could not consent to these uncertain modifications, but the President directed that a preliminary paper or protocol, as it is called, should be drawn up stating the terms upon which the United States would make peace with Spain.

The terms of this protocol were as follows: first, that Spain should leave Cuba; second, that Spain should give up to the United States Porto Rico and other West India islands, and also "an island in the Ladrones to be selected by the United States" — that meant Guam, of course; third, that Spain relinquish to the United States the temporary possession of the city, bay, and harbor of Manila, until the final treaty of peace should decide as to the disposition and control of the Philippines; fourth, that commissioners appointed by the United States and Spain should meet at once in Havana and San Juan, to arrange for and carry out the evacuation of the West Indies by Spain; fifth, that five American and five Spanish commissioners should be selected to meet in Paris, and draw up a definite treaty of peace; sixth, that upon the signing of this protocol, hostilities between Spain and the United States should be suspended.

This protocol showed the extent and emphasis of the American demands, and told Spain also what the war was to cost her in loss of prestige and possession. She would have hesitated, objected, and delayed, but American vigor opposed Spanish procrastination, and, with Yankee fleets and Yankee armies ready to enforce the American demands, the Spanish government yielded, and, on the twelfth of August, 1898, the protocol was signed in Washington by the Secretary of State for the United States, and the ambassador of France in behalf of Spain.

On that very day, August 21, the President issued his proclamation suspending hostilities, and the news sped over the telegraph wires to wherever in all the world the Spaniard and the American faced each other in fight.

If we agree to the accepted date and count the war to have begun at noon on April 12, it had lasted, up to the signing of the protocol on August 12, just one hundred and thirteen days. It had been a brief but a vigorous war. It had cost Spain two fleets and an army, while in Cuba and Porto Rico and the Philippines three other armies were cornered and practically conquered. With no help to be expected from her European neighbors, and no way to reënforce her garrisons and armies in her Atlantic or her Pacific colonies, there was but one alternative for Spain — surrender; and that she accepted.

You have seen how the news of peace came to our soldiers in Cuba and Porto Rico. It came in due time, as fast as the despatch boat from Hong Kong could carry it, to our victorious soldiers and sailors in distant Manila, and it came, bringing varied emotions, to the great army of reserves

BRIDGE ON THE EL CANEY ROAD.
(Spanning a creek on the way from Santiago.)

held for possible necessities in camps throughout the South. Those boys of the reserves, though never called upon to leave their home land for service on foreign shores, were yet as patriotic in their purposes and as worthy of praise and appreciation as were the heroes who rushed the lines at El Caney and stormed the heights of San Juan, or, who, on the far-off Asiatic beach, swarmed over the ramparts of the conquered Malate fort.

As the news of the suspension of hostilities sped over land and sea, the rigors of war at once relaxed. The armies of invasion stacked their guns and awaited orders; the blockade of Cuban and Porto Rican shores was raised, and in less than a week after the signing of the protocol the armies began to disband. On the eighteenth of August nearly one hundred thousand volunteers were ordered to be mustered out of service, and before the close of the year nearly one-half of the two hundred and fifty thousand soldiers called for had been discharged and returned to private life with the thanks and approval of the President at whose call they had rushed to arms and of the country whose interests they had so nobly volunteered to defend.

"It is fitting," said President McKinley, "that I should bear testimony to the patriotism and devotion of that large portion of our army which, although eager to be ordered to the post of greatest exposure, fortunately was not required outside of the United States. They did their whole duty, and like their comrades at the front have earned the gratitude of the nation. In like manner the officers and men of the army and of the navy

HOW THE WAR ENDED

who remained in their departments and stations faithfully performing most important duties connected with the war, and whose requests for assignment in the field and at sea I was compelled to refuse because their services were indispensable here, are entitled to the highest commendation." Indeed, it is true that, as Milton says in his noblest sonnet: —

> "They also serve who only stand and wait."

When the first note of peace came to the boys in the trenches and the camps before Santiago, sickness, that deadliest ally of war, had already laid its cruel and relentless hand upon the American army. The peril of a Cuban summer, greater than that of Mauser bullet and rapid-firing gun, had commenced its enervating work.

When General Shafter had been ordered to Cuba for a "quick campaign," he had reckoned upon this risk of sickness; for typhoid, malaria, and "yellow Jack" are the surest of all opponents to the tropical invasion. History had proved this, at Cartagena, in San Domingo, and Havana long years before. "Let the Yankees come," General Weyler, the Spaniard, said. "We won't need to fight them; fever will do our work for us."

IN SANTIAGO.
(A street corner and watering place near the cathedral.)

It seemed, after the excitement of surrender and of peace proposals had relaxed, that "General Weyler's ally" was to undo the victories and weaken the protocol of the triumphant Americans. Even before the destruction of Cervera's fleet, while yet the Americans held the heights they had stormed, the foe that none may fight had stolen into the camp of the conquerors. And after the victories still it came unbidden.

"The sickness among the troops," says General Shafter, "was increasing every day." Fever was in the American lines, and in the absence of sufficient medicine, good food, and adequate hospital service the trouble grew until alike the general and his officers saw that salvation meant immediate action. They so notified the War Department, and as speedily as possible the army in Cuba was sent north, where, in the health-giving breezes of Camp Wikoff, amid the sand-dunes of Montauk Point, health and strength slowly returned to the heroes of Santiago.

But not alone on Cuban heroes did fever lay its hand. The hateful touch fell also on every southern camp where northern boys, cared for by inexperience, and too often heedless of consequences, wilted beneath the strength-destroying clutch of typhoid and malaria. For three hundred men slain in battle, three thousand died in camp from fever and its kindred diseases. Wherever responsibility rests for this death-roll and for the sapping of strength which, in thousands of unreported cases, will linger in the blood through many a year, it is certain that the experience, though dearly bought, will not have been in vain, and that future campaigns in tropical lands — should such ever occur — will be better arranged for in the start, and more wisely conducted in details.

"One of the lessons taught by the war," says the report of the commission appointed to investigate the conduct of the War Department, "is that the country should hereafter be in a better state of preparation for war. Suggestions have been made that large supplies of all material not liable to deterioration should be kept on hand to be continuously issued and renewed, so that in any emergency they might be available. Especially should this be the case with such supplies as cannot be rapidly obtained in open market."

It was in transportation and supplies that the conduct of the war was especially lacking, while bad food is the worst of all evils; but should occasion again arise, no such deficiencies can be repeated if but the republic, without seeking to find a scapegoat for mismanagement, makes mismanagement impossible by a combination of the long-discussed "preparedness" and the recollection that "eternal vigilance is the price of liberty" — and of success, as well.

But outside the doleful record of illness and disease — less in proportion in this war than in any other of ancient or modern times — our "casualty roll" of the war with Spain in 1898 is peculiarly gratifying in its modesty. The total of these casualties was: Officers killed, 23; enlisted men, 257; total, 280; officers wounded, 113; enlisted men wounded, 1464; total, 1577. Of the navy: Killed, 17; wounded, 67; died as result of wounds, 1; invalided from service, 6; total, 91 — a total of less than seventeen hundred men.

AT MONTAUK.

("Surgeon's call" on the sick boys at Camp Wikoff.)

"It will be observed," says the President in his summing up, "that while our navy was engaged in two great battles and in numerous perilous undertakings in blockade and bombardment, and more than fifty thousand of our troops were transported to distant lands, and were engaged in assault and siege and battle and many skirmishes in unfamiliar territory, we lost in both arms of the service a total of 1668 killed and wounded, and in the entire campaign by land and sea we did not lose a gun, or a flag, or a transport, or a ship, and with the exception of the crew of the *Merrimac*, not a soldier or sailor was taken prisoner. On August 7, forty-six days from the date of the landing of General Shafter's army in Cuba, and twenty-one days from the surrender of Santiago, the United States troops commenced embarkation for home, and our entire force was returned to the United States as early as August 24. They were absent from the United States only two months."

On the ninth of September the President named the five members of the Peace Commission; the next day the Spanish government selected its five representatives, and the first business meeting of the joint Peace Commission was held in Paris on the first day of October. For two months the terms of the treaty were proposed, gone over, discussed, combated, declined, or accepted, in true diplomatic manner, while America chafed and fretted over what it deemed red tape and unnecessary delay. But diplomacy was never hasty, and Spain yielded small points slowly.

At length, however, it yielded completely. On November 28 Spain accepted the terms of the United States, which were those embodied in the original protocol of August 12. By the treaty Spain agreed to cede the Philippines to the United States upon a payment of twenty millions of dollars as "reimbursement for insular expenses"; also to cede to the United States Porto Rico, a few small West Indian islands, and Guam in the Ladrone group; and, finally, to abdicate its sovereignty in Cuba.

For this last clause the United States had gone to war with Spain; for it her fleets had sailed, her armies marched, battles by sea and land had been fought and won, and when, on the tenth of December, the treaty was signed at Paris by the commissioners of Spain and the United States, the cause for which the war was fought was won. Cuba was liberated; humanity had conquered; oppression was driven from the American continent.

On the twelfth of December American troops marched through the streets of Havana; on the sixteenth Fitzhugh Lee, the vigilant consul-general who had stood to the last for humanity and American rights, returned in triumph at the head of his soldiers to the city that had driven him out; on the twenty-eighth Cuba was evacuated by the Spanish troops, returned to their homes at America's expense; and on the first day of January, 1899, the Stars and Stripes floated in occupation above the palace of the governor-general in Havana, and America assumed temporary sovereignty in Cuba, to give it up to the Cubans themselves as agreed, when the Cubans themselves proved ready for stable self-government. Four hundred years of oppression were brought to a glorious end; Cuba was liberated; the *Maine* was avenged.

The treaty of peace went to the Senate for ratification; for, according to our Constitution, the Senate must pass upon and approve every such important document before the President affixes his signature. For days it stayed there under discussion, as arguments for or against it were made by senators, patriotic Americans all, but divided as the burdens of the future, growing from success, rose before them.

The main questions as to Cuban adjustment seemed to be lost in the more serious one of the occupation and disposition of the Philippines; for,

HOW THE WAR ENDED

after the surrender of Manila, the native Filipinos, led by their chief spirit, Aguinaldo, were displaying a hostility to American possession that grew more threatening as the ratification of the treaty was delayed.

The administration took the ground that, as our dealings had been with Spain, whom we had dispossessed, we had no right or reason to recognize and yield to the Filipinos, or even to consider their claims, until the island had been pacified, and Congress, when the treaty with Spain had been ratified, decided upon our future action.

Our success in the Philippines, as I have already told you, brought us face to face with a duty that was a difficulty. This duty we could not escape; its responsibilities we could not shirk. We were confronting "not a theory but a condition." Every American, exercising his free prerogative, could criticise or advise. But one thing was certain: until the treaty was ratified we could not act. As the President explained, "we could not discharge the responsibilities upon us until these islands became ours either by conquest or treaty; there was but one alternative, and that was either Spain or the United States in the Philippines."

So an army and navy waited for the action of the Senate. At last, on Monday, the sixth of February, 1899, the decisive vote came and the treaty with Spain was ratified by a vote of fifty-seven to twenty-nine. The President signed the important document, and the war with Spain was ended.

The very day before the ratification, on Sunday, the fifth of February, the insurgent army around Manila made an unprovoked attack upon the American troops. A series of battles ensued in which once again the valor of the American soldier, directed by the genius of General Otis, and the watchfulness of the American navy still marshalled by the cool-headed Admiral Dewey, came out victorious, and the misguided and ill-advised Filipinos were defeated again and again.

Sympathy for a people struggling for independence is an American trait; for through blood and tears did America battle for and win her priceless boon of liberty. But until peace and order had been secured in the Philippines, as in Cuba, we could not yield to unwise demands nor recognize an unstable authority. The contest with Spain was not for aggrandizement or empire; it was for humanity, and no consent is needed to perform an act of humanity.

The wise President who, against his will, had chosen the stern arbitrament of war, himself has solemnly declared that "the Philippines, like Cuba and Porto Rico, were intrusted to our hands by the war, and to that great trust, under the providence of God and in the name of human progress and civilization, we are committed. It is a trust we have not sought; it is a trust from which we will not flinch."

"That the inhabitants of the Philippines," he said, "will be benefited by this republic is my unshaken belief. That they will have a kindlier government under our guidance and that they will be aided in every possible way to be a self-respecting and self-governing people is as true as that the American people love liberty and have an abiding faith in their own institutions.

"No imperial designs lurk in the American mind. They are alien to American sentiment, thought, and purpose. Our priceless principles undergo no change under a tropical sun. They go with the flag. They are wrought in every one of its sacred folds, and are indistinguishable as its shining stars.

"'Why read ye not the changeless truth,
The free can conquer but to save.'"

The free have conquered, and the free will save: Cuba and the Philippines will be regenerated in spite of themselves, and the blood of our heroes will not have flowed in vain. The work of Waring and of Wood, the martyr and the hero alike of peace and war, will work grand results, and cleanliness, which is next to godliness, will restore the fever-ridden island to its original healthfulness and fertility. This redemption, however, may not be accomplished speedily or in the peaceful way we desire. But it will surely be accomplished, and, as the President said: —

"If we can benefit these remote peoples, who will object? If, in the years of the future, they are established in government under law and liberty, who will regret our perils and sacrifices? Who will not rejoice in our heroism and humanity? Always perils, and always after them safety; always darkness and clouds, but always shining through them the light and the sunshine; always cost and sacrifice, but always after them the fruition of liberty, education, and civilization."

So our war with Spain, which began because of duty, ends with an even greater duty; a war begun in the cause of humanity to answer a bitter cry for help too long ignored, ends in a prob-

HOW THE WAR ENDED

lem from which the doubter and the alarmist would shrink, but which the true American will boldly face — the problem of how America shall act in the opportunity for progress and for the widening of her circles of influence and civilization in the world. Our fathers never shirked responsibility; shall their sons fear to face the future boldly and bravely? Listen to the Englishman's advice, born of generations of such responsibility, — Kipling, the latest laureate of the Anglo-Saxon: —

> "Take up the White Man's burden —
> Have done with childish days —
> The lightly proffered laurel,
> The easy, ungrudged praise;
> Comes now to search your manhood
> Through all the thankless years,
> Cold, edged with dear-bought wisdom,
> The judgment of your peers."

We can meet the "judgment of our peers" unfalteringly. Despite shortcomings, unpreparedness, and needless distress, we won our victory and liberated a people. War is always deplorable, and this war was no exception. It cost America millions of money and thousands of brave lives; it cost sickness and suffering and sorrow. But, as Professor Williams gloriously sums it up,

"All priceless things cost something. Civilization has cost something. Christianity cost something. Let us have done with carping! No war in all history, measured in proportion to its magnificent results, — if we would but see them, — cost so little as the Spanish war of 1898. No such great stage in the development of the human race has cost so little in life and suffering."

It has brought us a higher manhood; it has given us a wider charity and a nobler sense of brotherhood. It has united the North and South; it has brought closer together the East and West. It has drawn the Anglo-Saxon kin on both sides the sea nearer to each other, and has secured one more triumph in the long, long struggle of liberty against oppression. It has compelled admiration for American valor on land and on sea, and advanced the flag for which Washington fought and Webster pleaded and Lincoln died; it has made Americans proud of their glorious birthright and has given a new and nobler meaning to the splendid and passionate appeal for "Liberty and Union, now and forever, one and inseparable!"

THE STORY OF
OUR WAR WITH SPAIN
CHRONOLOGICALLY TOLD

[1895–1899]

THE CHRONOLOGICAL STORY OF OUR WAR WITH SPAIN

From the Outbreak of the Rebellion to the Treaty of Peace

(Reprinted by permission of the Boston *Transcript*.)

1895.

February 24. — Insurrection breaks out in three of Cuba's six provinces.

March 31. — General Antonio Maceo proclaimed commander of the insurgent army.

April 14. — Captain-General Cajelia displaced by Campos.

November 17. — General Maceo, near Santa Clara, with 1900 men defeats 2800 Spanish troops.

1896.

February 10. — Weyler displaces Captain-General Campos.

February 12. — Eighteen thousand new Spanish troops sent into the field.

February 17. — Weyler issues his reconcentrado proclamations.

March 1. — The trocha is established.

April 11. — Maceo crosses the trocha with 3000 men and drives back the Spanish.

October 1. — The rebellion up to this time has cost Spain $230,000,000.

December 4. — General Antonio Maceo killed by treachery.

December 10. — General Ruiz Rivera succeeds Maceo.

1897.

August 8. — Premier Canovas of Spain assassinated.

October 2. — Weyler recalled by the Sagasta liberal ministry on pressure from the United States.

November 27. — Decree from government at Madrid granting autonomy to Cuba.

1898.

January 24. — United States battleship *Maine* ordered to Havana on a peaceful mission.

February 10. — De Lome, Spanish minister, recalled for unwarranted personalities reflecting on President McKinley.

February 15. — The destruction of the *Maine* in the harbor of Havana was the first and great catastrophe experienced by the United States in all her dealings with Spain. At twenty minutes before 10 o'clock in the evening, an explosion occurred, by which the entire forward part of the vessel was destroyed. Two officers and 264 of the crew perished, those who were not killed outright by the explosion being pinned between decks by the tangle of wreckage and drowned by the immediate sinking of the hull. The days which followed were days of anxious suspense. A wave of indignation swept over the length and breadth of the land. Captain Sigsbee's message asking that judgment be suspended did not altogether reassure the people. A great cry for vengeance arose. The more impressionable openly criticised the President's calmness.

February 17. — The following officers were appointed to investigate the cause of the *Maine* disaster: Captain W. T. Sampson of the *Iowa*, president; Captain F. E. Chadwick of the *New York;*

Lieutenant-Commander W. P. Potter of the *New York*, with Lieutenant-Commander Adolf Marix of the *Vermont*, as recorders.

February 18. — Spanish cruiser *Vizcaya* arrives at New York.

February 19. — Spain's request for a joint investigation of the *Maine* affair refused.

March 9. — Congress passes the $50,000,000 national defence bill.

March 16. — The remonstrance of the Spanish government against our measures of defence and the presence of our fleet at Key West was received.

March 28. — President McKinley sent to Congress the report of the United States Board of Inquiry. This document was dated March 21, and contained the information that the *Maine* had been destroyed through the agency of a submarine mine. It did not fix the blame.

April 7. — Diplomatic representatives of Germany, Austria-Hungary, France, Great Britain, Italy, and Russia presented a joint communication to President McKinley on behalf of the European Powers, in which was expressed a hope that affairs between the United States and Spain would be amicably adjusted. President McKinley's reply, couched in conciliatory language, was rather negative in its import.

April 9. — Consul-General Lee and other Americans leave Cuba.

April 11. — The President sends a message to Congress recommending armed intervention in Cuba.

April 15. — War Department orders regular troops to the coast.

April 16. — The intervention resolution passed by the Senate.

April 19. — The President prepares an ultimatum to Spain demanding the evacuation of Cuba within three days.

April 20. — The Cuban resolutions signed by the President.

April 20. — The United States government sent its ultimatum to Spain. The demand was made that Spain should, before the hour of noon of April 23, withdraw her forces from Cuba. Señor

Bernabe, the Spanish minister, at once requested his passports and started immediately for Canada. In Madrid the Cortes convened, and the Queen Regent delivered an address, appealing to the Spanish people to defend their rights.

April 21. — General Woodford, United States minister to Madrid, given his passports. The United States held this severance of diplomatic relations to be a declaration of war.

April 21. — Captain William T. Sampson made acting admiral of the North Atlantic squadron, with the cruiser *New York* as his flagship.

April 22. — North Atlantic squadron sails to blockade Cuban ports.

April 22. — First shot fired, when the United States gunboat *Nashville* captured the Spanish Gulf steamer *Buena Ventura*.

April 22. — President's proclamation to all nations declaring the blockade of Cuban ports.

April 23. — The President's call issued for 125,000 volunteers.

April 26. — President's proclamation issues on Spanish vessels in United States ports.

April 27. — Asiatic squadron sails from Mirs Bay (having been ordered from Hong Kong by Great Britain in compliance with neutrality law) to meet the Spanish fleet at the Philippine Islands.

April 27. — First hostile shot of the war: United States cruisers *New York* and *Cincinnati* and monitor *Puritan* silence the batteries at Matanzas.

April 29. — Spanish fleet left Cape Verde Islands, being Spain's first move against the United States.

May 1. — This day witnessed the greatest naval victory in the history of the world. The people of the United States were electrified by the news that the entire Spanish fleet commanded by Admiral Montojo had been destroyed by Commodore Dewey in Manila Bay, and that the feat had been accomplished without serious injury to any of our ships and no loss of life on the American side.

CHRONOLOGICALLY TOLD 343

May 2. — Congress appropriated $35,720,945 for the army of invasion.

May 2. — Naval bill for thirty-five new warships sent to the President for signature.

May 7. — Commodore Dewey's report on battle of Manila received. Eleven Spanish warships destroyed, and no Americans killed.

May 7. — The President in the name of the American people congratulates Commodore Dewey.

May 9. — Commodore Dewey is made rear-admiral.

May 11. — Ensign Bagley and four men on gunboat *Winslow* killed in engagement off Cardenas.

May 12. — Admiral Sampson's fleet shells forts and land batteries at San Juan, Porto Rico.

May 17. — United States establishes censorship on press despatches.

May 18. — A new Spanish cabinet is formed.

May 20. — Secretary Long officially confirms report of Spanish fleet off Santiago de Cuba.

May 21. — General Merritt sails for Manila.

May 25. — President calls for 75,000 more volunteers.

May 26. — Battleship *Oregon* arrives at Key West after a cruise of 17,499 miles from San Francisco, a most notable feat.

May 29. — Commodore Schley locates Cervera at Santiago.

June 1. — Admiral Sampson relieves Commodore Schley at Santiago.

June 3. — Lieutenant Hobson and his men sink the *Merrimac* near the channel at Santiago.

June 4. — The Senate passed the war revenue bill.

June 4. — Captain Gridley of the *Olympia* died in Kobe, Japan, on his way home.

June 6. — American marines land at Aguadores and Daiquiri.

June 6. — Second bombardment of the forts at Santiago.

June 6. — Insurgents take outer city of Manila and 18,000 Spanish prisoners.

June 7. — United States fleet bombards and destroys the fortifications at Caimanera.

June 7. — The *Monterey* sails from San Francisco to Manila.

June 9. — Fortifications at Guantanamo Bay destroyed.

June 11. — American marines land at Guantanamo.

June 12. — First battle of Guantanamo. Four American marines killed.

June 14. — General Shafter and army of 16,000 men sail from Tampa.

June 15. — The second relief expedition sails for the Philippines.

June 22. — The *St. Paul* cripples the *Terror* off San Juan in Porto Rico.

June 22. — General Shafter's army lands at Daiquiri.

June 24. — Two thousand Spaniards attack one thousand American Rough Riders and regulars. Spaniards repulsed. American loss, sixteen.

June 27. — Commodore Watson's fleet ordered to prepare for expedition to the coast of Spain.

June 27. — Admiral Camara's fleet at Port Said refused coal by the Egyptian government.

June 28. — Third Manila expedition sails.

June 30. — American troops move upon the city of Santiago.

July 2. — The two most important engagements of the Cuban campaign fell upon this day, both being successful, although the American forces met with heavy losses. General Lawton's infantry stormed the hills of Caney, the Seventh, Twelfth, and Seventeenth infantry (General Chaffee's brigade) leading in the attack. In the taking of San Juan the unmounted cavalry, the First and Tenth regulars, and Roosevelt's Rough Riders bore the brunt of the fighting, again distinguishing themselves and adding fresh laurels to those already won at Las Guasimas. Our

CHRONOLOGICALLY TOLD

losses in these two engagements were 23 officers and 208 men killed and 81 officers and 1203 wounded. These figures are from General Shafter's report.

July 3. — Admiral Cervera's fleet destroyed by Commodore Schley. The *Infanta Maria Teresa*, *Oquendo*, and *Vizcaya* were forced ashore, burned, and blown up within twenty miles of Santiago. The *Furor* and *Pluton* were destroyed within four miles of port. Our loss, one killed and two wounded. Enemy's loss probably several hundred from gun fire, explosions, and drowning. About twelve hundred prisoners, including Admiral Cervera. The American killed was G. H. Ellis, chief yeoman of the *Brooklyn*.

July 3. — Guam of the Ladrone islands seized by the Americans.

July 4. — First relief expedition reaches Admiral Dewey.

July 6. — Spanish prisoners en route to Portsmouth, N.H., on the *Harvard*, mutiny and several are shot.

July 7. — General Miles starts for Santiago — Lieutenant Hobson and his men are exchanged.

July 8. — Santiago given formal notice of twenty-four hours before bombardment.

July 9. — Admiral Camara's fleet returns through the Suez Canal to Spain.

July 9. — Major-General Miles leaves with reënforcements for Santiago.

July 10. — General Shafter and Admiral Sampson begin the bombardment of Santiago.

July 11. — Several deaths from yellow fever reported in the American camps.

July 11. — Armistice agreed for twenty-four hours at Santiago.

July 12. — The Spanish cabinet resigns.

July 14. — General Toral formally surrendered Santiago and troops and garrison in eastern Cuba.

July 15. — Commissioners agree on details of terms of surrender.

July 15. — General McKibbon named as temporary military governor of Santiago.

July 16. — Garrison and city of Caimanera formally surrender.

July 17. — With formal ceremonies the American flag is hoisted over the public buildings of Santiago.

July 20. — Colonel Wood of the Rough Riders (United States First Volunteer Cavalry) made military governor of Santiago.

July 20. — General Miles started from Guantanamo for Porto Rico with an army of invasion.

July 20. — Underbidding a pool of American liners, the Compania Transatlantica Española obtained contracts for transporting Spanish prisoners home from Santiago.

July 20. — Permanent annexation of Porto Rico announced as the policy of the Administration.

July 20. — Spanish cabinet informed by Blanco that he did not authorize General Toral's surrender.

July 25. — General Miles lands at Guanico, Porto Rico.

July 26. — M. Jules Cambon, the French ambassador at Washington, at the request of the Spanish Minister of Foreign Affairs, conveyed to President McKinley a message which first opened the way to peace negotiations. A request was made for terms under which the United States would be willing to end the war.

July 26. — Americans advance on Port Ponce. Spanish loss, three killed, twelve wounded. American loss, four wounded.

July 27. — Port of Ponce invested. Seventy lighters captured.

July 28. — City of Ponce and town of Port Ponce under American military government.

July 30. — The French ambassador, M. Cambon, asks for terms of peace.

August 1. — United States terms of peace received and considered by cabinet in Madrid.

CHRONOLOGICALLY TOLD 347

August 3. — The President receives unofficial advices that Spain has accepted peace terms offered.

August 4. — Three thousand Spanish troops attack Americans under General Greene, intrenched near Manila and are repulsed with heavy loss.

August 4. — General Shafter's army at Santiago receives orders to come north.

August 6. — Madrid despatches say Spanish cabinet's agreement to peace conditions has been drafted and presented to the Queen Regent for approval.

August 8–10. — General Miles's army continues its advance toward San Juan de Porto Rico, Spaniards offering but slight opposition.

August 11. — The Spanish government approved the protocol and cabled to M. Cambon, at Washington, to sign the preliminaries of peace.

August 12. — M. Cambon received his instructions on behalf of Spain at one o'clock. At exactly twenty-three minutes past 4 P.M. his signature and that of the Secretary of State were affixed. The President at once issued a proclamation declaring a suspension of hostilities, and messages to that effect were despatched to General Miles in Porto Rico, to General Merritt in the Philippines, and to General Shafter at Santiago. Similar advices were cabled Admirals Sampson and Dewey. One hour before the document was signed a bombardment of Manzanillo, province of Santiago, was begun by the *Newark*, *Hist*, *Suwanee*, *Osceola*, and *Alvarado*. It was not until early the next morning (August 13) that the message reached Captain Goodrich of the *Newark*. In Porto Rico news of peace stopped a battle at Arbonito and Pablo Vasques, just in the nick of time.

August 13. — The attack upon Manila by Dewey and Merritt began. A division of the squadron shelled the forts at Malate, on the south side of the city, while the trenches were stormed by the land forces. The squadron had no casualties, and no vessels were injured. The Spaniards were driven back by Merritt's men and retreated into the walled city, where resistance was useless. General Jaudenes agreed to surrender, and General Merritt went to the palace, where the Spaniards laid down their arms.

August 17. — The adjutant-general cabled to General Merritt: "The President directs that there must be no joint occupation with the insurgents." Merritt issued a proclamation to the people of the Philippines.

August 24. — Mustering-out of volunteers begins.

August 30. — General Merritt leaves Manila for Paris.

August 31. — Spanish prisoners at Portsmouth, N.H., released.

September 8. — Secretary of War Alger requested the President to appoint a commission to investigate the conduct of the War Department.

September 9. — The President named the following-named gentlemen to constitute the Peace Commission: William R. Day, Cushman K. Davis, William P. Frye, Whitelaw Reid, and George Gray.

September 17. — Spanish Peace Commission appointed with these members: Montero Rios, General Cerero, Señor Abnarzura, Señor Villarrutie, Señor Garnica. American commissioners sail from New York.

September 21. — American commissioners reach Liverpool.

September 27. — American and Spanish commissioners reach Paris.

October 1. — First business meeting of the Peace Commissions.

October 18. — Porto Rico evacuated; General Brooke appointed governor-general.

October 21. — Spain agrees to assume the Cuban debt.

October 21. — Spanish commissioners notified that the United States will take all the Philippines.

November 4. — Spain refuses to accept American Philippine proposals.

November 12. — Spain asks time to reply.

November 21. — Ultimatum presented to Spain. Twenty million dollars offered for the Philippines. Forged despatch sent from Paris announcing withdrawal of Señor Rios, head of the Spanish Commission.

November 25. — Spain's offer to sell the Philippines to the United States for $100,000,000 refused.

November 28. — Spain accepts the terms of the United States to cede the Philippines to America for $20,000,000 (reimbursement for insular expenses); also to cede Guam and Porto Rico and to abdicate sovereignty of Cuba.

December 10. — Peace treaty signed at Paris.

December 12. — The 202d New York marches through the streets of Havana.

December 13. — General Brooke appointed governor-general of Cuba.

December 16. — Consul-General Lee returns to Cuba.

December 24. — Peace treaty presented to the President.

December 25. — Rioting in Havana suburbs.

December 28. — Cuba evacuated by the Spaniards, save a few troops in Matanzas and Cienfuegos.

1899

January 1. — Americans take possession of Cuba.

February 6. — The United States Senate ratifies and the President signs the treaty of peace with Spain.

March 3. — Dewey made admiral of the navy.

March 17. — Queen Regent of Spain signs the treaty of peace.

www.ingramcontent.com/pod-product-compliance
Lightning Source LLC
Chambersburg PA
CBHW032016230426
43671CB00005B/105